New England Historic Genealogical Society

Rolls of Membership of the New-England Historic Genealogical

Society

1844-1891

New England Historic Genealogical Society

Rolls of Membership of the New-England Historic Genealogical Society
1844-1891

ISBN/EAN: 9783337845216

Printed in Europe, USA, Canada, Australia, Japan

Cover: Foto ©Andreas Hilbeck / pixelio.de

More available books at **www.hansebooks.com**

Rolls of Membership

OF THE

NEW-ENGLAND

HISTORIC GENEALOGICAL SOCIETY

1844–1891

BOSTON
PRINTED FOR THE SOCIETY
1892

University Press:
JOHN WILSON AND SON, CAMBRIDGE.

PREFACE.

UPON the re-organization of the Society, in January, 1889, the newly-elected Council was confronted with many important matters which pressed for attention. These are enumerated in the President's Address to the Council on 14 January, 1889, which was referred to a Committee, of which the Rev. Andrew P. Peabody, D.D., LL.D., was Chairman. Acting upon the recommendation of that Committee, the Council passed the following order on 5 February, 1889 : —

Ordered, That a Special Committee of three members of the Society be appointed, to be known as the Committee on the Rolls of Membership, whose duty it shall be to prepare complete lists, in chronological and alphabetical order, of the names of all persons that have ever been actually members of this Society, and to submit said lists to the Council, with such recommendations as they may deem expedient.

The Committee at once addressed itself to its work, and during the three years and more which have since elapsed has labored assiduously to discharge faithfully the arduous duty assigned to it. The existing manuscript and printed Lists of Members proved, on inspection, to be so thoroughly untrustworthy that they were cast aside, and the enumeration here presented was made *de novo* from the manuscript records of the Society. This laborious part of the Committee's work was undertaken by Mr. Clarke, who also conducted an extensive correspondence, by which many obscure points were made clear, and the full name of every member of the Society recovered and preserved.

Mr. Edes has had entire charge of the press, and is the responsible Editor of the Rolls after they left Mr. Clarke's hands. The List of Officers, 1845–1892, was compiled by Mr. Edes ; and the Indexes of Officers, Members, and Places have been made under his personal supervision and at his private expense.

Dr. Brown has paid attention especially to that part of the work which dealt with the academic honors of our members : and none but his associates know how difficult and perplexing his task has been.

The Librarians of the principal Colleges in the New-England and
Middle States have taken great interest in this work, and have rendered
much and valuable aid. Mr. Charles A. Cutter of the Boston Athe-
naeum, Mr. William H. Tillinghast of the Harvard College Library,
Mr. Edmund M. Barton of the American Antiquarian Society, and Mr.
John M. Comstock, Editor of the Dartmouth College General Catalogue,
have been unceasing in their courtesies and in kind attention to constant
inquiries. Not a few members of the Society, and especially Mr. John
Ward Dean, Mr. William Blake Trask, the Rev. Edmund Farwell
Slafter, D.D., and Mr. Benjamin Barstow Torrey, have materially aided
the Committee in its work; while the service rendered by Mr. Henry
Ernest Woods, the efficient Secretary of the Library Committee, has
been so constant, intelligent, and indispensable, and his interest so
persistent, that the Committee cannot refrain from recording here its
cordial appreciation and its special acknowledgment of his work.

To one other of our Fellows, the Society as well as the Committee
owes a lasting debt of gratitude. Had it not been for his generous and
genuine interest in this undertaking it would have been impossible to
present results at all comparable with the Committee's completed work.
Mr. John Wilson placed at our service the entire resources of the
University Press. When it is remembered that these Rolls bear nearly
three thousand names, that they are here printed entirely in capital
letters, and that all were put in type at once, and kept standing for
more than a year without extra charge to the Society, the extent of those
resources and the value of Mr. Wilson's contribution to this work, which
has had his personal supervision throughout, will be readily understood
and appreciated.

In the autumn of 1889 the Council granted the Committee on the
Rolls leave to report in print. In order to avail of the criticism of
subscribers and readers of the REGISTER before printing the Rolls in the
form in which they are now presented, the Council passed the following
order on 2 February, 1891 : —

Ordered, That the Committee on Printing and Stationery cause to be
printed . . . the Rolls of Membership of the Society, said Rolls to be pub-
lished in whole or in part, either in the REGISTER or in a separate publication
or both, as the said Committee shall determine.

The Resident Roll appeared in the April (1891) number of the
REGISTER, the Honorary Roll and the Corresponding Roll in the July
number, and the Indexes in the October number. Extra copies of the
Rolls were sent to prominent persons, well qualified for such service, in

Europe as well as in various parts of the United States, inviting their criticism and corrections. The responses were prompt and the corrections numerous and valuable, and vindicate the wisdom of the order providing for the tentative publication.

In 1870-71 a subscription of about $15,000 was raised to buy and remodel the Society's House in Somerset Street. Of the subscribers many who were not previously members of the Society were admitted to Resident Membership. At the Stated Meeting, held 6 April, 1870, on motion of Mr. William B. Towne, the following vote was passed, which accounts for the unusually large number of accessions to the list of Life Members during that period : —

Voted, That all Resident Members who have or may contribute the sum of one hundred dollars or upwards to the Building or Publication Fund of this Society shall be enrolled Life Members, and shall ever after be exempt from annual assessment.

On 31 March, 1874, the Board of Directors, by resolution, declared Cyrus Wakefield, Isaac Rich, M. Day Kimball, and Theron J. Dale, subscribers to the Building Fund, — all of whom had deceased before accepting in writing their Election as Resident Members, as required by the Constitution, — to have been Resident Members. This action has been generally regarded by those who had cognizance of it as illegal ; the Committee, being unanimously of the same opinion, has omitted their names from the Roll.

The present code of By-Laws, adopted 2 May, 1888, makes no provision for a separate class of Life Members : but under it Resident Members may commute their Annual Dues by the payment at one time of Thirty Dollars. Those members who have availed of this privilege are indicated in the Rolls by the expression " Fees Commuted." The present code also provides that Resident Members removing from New England, and Corresponding Members removing into New England shall cease to be Members. This provision, however, has been declared by the Council to be not retroactive. Under some former codes the provision for forfeiture was either different or lacking, consequently the names of a few persons residing in New England will still be found among those of our oldest living Corresponding Members ; and the Resident Roll bears the names of others who live beyond the borders of New England.

The Rolls as here presented are believed to contain the name of every person who has ever been a member of the Society prior to 1 January, 1892, with the date of his election. As these Rolls are intended to be an official record, it seemed to the Committee proper to append to each name all the academic degrees to which the bearer of it was entitled, except A.B. when followed by A.M., and D.B. when followed by D.D. In the Honorary Roll and the Corresponding Roll, an attempt has been made to indicate such of the principal learned Society honors conferred upon our members as can be expressed by initial letters. This course, for various reasons, has not been practicable in dealing with the Resident Roll. The title of "Reverend" is appended in parentheses to the names of clergymen who have not received the degree of D.B. or D.D. The titles of "Honorable" and "Esquire" and military and naval titles are omitted, except that officers of the regular Army and Navy are designated by the proper initials.

All Residences are in Massachusetts unless the contrary is stated, and are those of members at the time of their election. Villages and Post-offices are not recognized, except those within the municipal limits of Boston.

Nearly forty years ago Mr. Henry Stevens wrote: "If you are troubled with a pride of accuracy and would have it completely taken out of you, print a catalogue." The Committee, while not unmindful of the truth of Mr. Stevens's observation, has spared no pains in its endeavor to approach as nearly as possible to an accurate and complete performance.

In conclusion, the Committee notes the gratifying fact that it is able to send forth these lists with the name of the venerable Dr. Lucius Robinson Paige, who was the first associate elected by the Founders of the Society, still standing at the head of the Resident Roll. Since 21 January, 1845, — a period of nearly half a century, — the honored name of Dr. Paige has dignified the fellowship of this Society, whose members hold him in reverent and affectionate regard.

GEORGE K. CLARKE,
HENRY H. EDES,
FRANCIS H. BROWN,

Committee on the Rolls of Membership.

18 SOMERSET STREET, BOSTON,
20 May, 1892.

OFFICERS OF THE SOCIETY.

1845-1892.

Presidents.

CHARLES EWER 1845-1850
JOSEPH BARLOW FELT (Rev.),
   LL.D. 1850-1853
WILLIAM WHITING, LL.D. . 1853-1858
SAMUEL GARDNER DRAKE,
   A.M. 1858-1859
ALMON DANFORTH HODGES . 1859-1861

WINSLOW LEWIS, M.D.. . . . 1861-1866
JOHN ALBION ANDREW, LL.D. 1866-1867
MARSHALL PINCKNEY WILDER,
   LL.D. 1868-1886
ABNER CHENEY GOODELL. Jr.,
   A.M. 1887

Vice-Presidents.

MASSACHUSETTS.

LEMUEL SHATTUCK 1845-1850
LUCIUS ROBINSON PAIGE, D.D. 1850-1851
NATHANIEL BRADSTREET
   SHURTLEFF, M.D. 1851-1853
TIMOTHY FARRAR. LL.D. . . 1853-1858
FRANCIS BRINLEY, A.M. . . 1858-1859
CHARLES HUDSON, A.M. . . 1859-1861
MARTIN MOORE (Rev.), A.M. 1861-1866
GEORGE BRUCE UPTON (Hon.) 1866-1874
GEORGE CARTER RICHARDSON
   (Hon.) 1875-1886
WILLIAM ENDICOTT, Jr., A.M. 1887-1892
BENJAMIN APTHORP GOULD,
   LL.D. 1892

MAINE.

WILLIAM WILLIS, LL.D. . . 1855-1859
JOHN APPLETON, LL.D. . . 1859-1865
ISRAEL WASHBURN, Jr., LL.D. 1865-1883
JOSEPH WILLIAMSON, A.M. . 1884

NEW HAMPSHIRE.

NOAH MARTIN, M.D. . . . 1855-1859
SAMUEL DANA BELL, LL.D. . 1859-1868
IRA PERLEY, LL.D. 1869-1874

WILLIAM BLANCHARD TOWNE.
   A.M. 1875-1876
ASA DODGE SMITH, D.D.,
   LL.D. 1877-1877
JOSEPH BURBEEN WALKER,
   A.M. 1878

VERMONT.

JOHN WHEELER, D.D. . . . 1855-1859
HENRY CLARK 1859-1867
HAMPDEN CUTTS. A.M. . . 1867-1875
HILAND HALL, LL.D. . . . 1875-1885
HORACE FAIRBANKS (Hon.) . 1886-1888
JAMES BARRETT. LL.D.. . . 1889

RHODE ISLAND.

WILLIAM READ STAPLES,
   LL.D.. 1855-1859
JOHN BARSTOW 1859-1864
USHER PARSONS, M.D.. . . 1864-1868
JOHN RUSSELL BARTLETT,
   A.M. 1869-1886
WILLIAM GAMMELL, LL.D. . 1887-1889
ELISHA BENJAMIN ANDREWS,
   D.D., LL.D. 1890

CONNECTICUT.

NATHANIEL GOODWIN (Hon.) 1855–1855
LEONARD BACON, D.D., LL.D. 1855–1859
FREDERICK WILLIAM CHAP-
  MAN (Rev.), A.M. 1859–1865
CALVIN ELLIS STOWE, D.D. . 1865–1869
WILLIAM ALFRED BUCKING-
  HAM, LL.D. 1869–1875

HENRY PHILEMON HAVEN
  (Hon.). 1876–1876
MARSHALL JEWELL, A.M. . . 1877–1883
EDWIN HOLMES BUGBEE
  (Hon.). 1884–1892
EDWARD ELBRIDGE SALISBURY,
  LL.D.. 1892

Honorary Vice-Presidents.

The Fifth Article of the Constitution, adopted 17 December, 1844, provided for one Vice-President. On 4 October, 1854, a new Article, providing for "a Vice-President for each of the New England States, and for such other of the United States as the Society may by vote determine," was adopted in place of Article 5, repealed. On 6 December, 1854, the Society voted that the Vice-Presidents for other than New-England States should be styled Honorary Vice-Presidents. The first plural election occurred 7 February, 1855. The office of Honorary Vice-President was abolished, 2 May, 1888, by the adoption of the present By-Laws.

UNITED STATES.

RUTHERFORD   BURCHARD
  HAYES,[1] LL.D. 1879–1882

CALIFORNIA.

ANDREW RANDALL 1856–1856
WILLIAM INGRAHAM KIP,
  D.D., LL.D. 1875–1889

DELAWARE.

CHARLES BRECK,[2] D.D. . . 1887–1889

DISTRICT OF COLUMBIA.

GEORGE PURNELL FISHER, A.B. 1864–1873
WILLIAM ADAMS RICHARDSON,
  LL.D.. 1873–1889

GEORGIA.

CHARLES COLCOCK JONES,
  LL.D. 1886–1889

ILLINOIS.

JOHN WENTWORTH, LL.D. . . { 1855–1876
                          { 1879–1888

INDIANA.

BALLARD SMITH, A.B. . . . 1856–1866
JOSEPH FARRAND TUTTLE,
  D.D., LL.D. 1868–1889

IOWA.

HENRY WASHINGTON LEE,
  D.D., LL.D. 1856–1874
WILLIAM STEVENS PERRY,
  D.D., D.C.L., LL.D. . . 1878–1889

LOUISIANA.

WILLARD FRANCIS MALLALIEU,
  D.D. 1886–1889

MARYLAND.

SEBASTIAN FERRIS STREETER,
  A.M. 1856–1864
JOHN HAZLEHURST BONNEVAL
  LATROBE (Hon.) 1865–1876
EDWIN AUGUSTIN DALRYMPLE,
  D.D. 1876–1881

MICHIGAN.

LEWIS CASS, LL.D. 1855–1866
HOVEY KILBURN CLARKE
  (Hon.) 1883–1889

MINNESOTA.

EDWARD DUFFIELD NEILL,
  D.D. 1883–1889

MISSOURI.

WILLIAM GREENLEAF ELIOT,
  D.D., LL.D. 1867–1887

[1] See Ohio.   [2] See Pennsylvania.

NEW JERSEY.

JOHN LAURIS BLAKE, D.D. . 1856-1857
JOSEPH COURTEN HORNBLOWER,
  LL.D. 1858-1864
SALOMON ALOFSEN 1865-1873
WILLIAM ADEE WHITEHEAD,
  A.M. 1873-1884
JOHN GILMARY SHEA, LL.D. . 1888-1889

NEW YORK.

MILLARD FILLMORE, LL.D. . 1855-1874
JOHN ADAMS DIX, LL.D. . . 1875-1879
ROBERT SAFFORD HALE, LL.D. 1881-1881
GEORGE WILLIAM CURTIS,
  LL.D. 1884-1889

NORTH CAROLINA.

EDWARD KIDDER . . . . { 1856-1863
            { 1883-1885
SILAS NELSON MARTIN (Hon.) 1876-1877

OHIO.

ELIJAH HAYWARD, A.B. . . 1855-1864
THOMAS SPOONER (Hon.) . . 1868-1882

RUTHERFORD BURCHARD
HAYES.[1] LL.D. 1882-1889

PENNSYLVANIA.

SAMUEL BRECK (Hon.) . . . 1856-1862
WILLIAM DARLINGTON, M.D..
  LL.D.. 1863-1863
NATHANIEL CHAUNCEY, A.M. 1863-1865
WILLIAM DUANE 1866-1882
CHARLES BRECK.[2] D.D. . . 1883-1887
WILLIAM HENRY EGLE, M.D. 1887-1889

SOUTH CAROLINA.

THOMAS SMYTH, D.D. . . . 1856-1863

VIRGINIA.

PHILIP SLAUGHTER, D.D. . . 1888-1889

WISCONSIN.

CYRUS WOODMAN, A.M. . . 1856-1864
INCREASE ALLEN LAPHAM,
  LL.D. 1864-1875
LYMAN COPELAND DRAPER,
  LL.D.. 1876-1889

Recording Secretaries.

JOHN WINGATE THORNTON,
  A.M. 1845-1846
SAMUEL HOPKINS RIDDEL
  (Rev.), A.M. 1846-1851
CHARLES MAYO 1851-1856
FRANCIS BRINLEY, A.M. . . 1856-1857
DAVID PULSIFER, A.M.. . . 1857-1857
JOHN WARD DEAN, A.M. . . 1857-1858
WILLIAM MASON CORNELL,
  M.D., D.D., LL.D. 1858-1859
CALEB DAVIS BRADLEE, D.D. 1859-1862

EDWARD FRANKLIN EVERETT,
  A.M. 1862-1863
EDWARD SPRAGUE RAND, Jr.,
  A.M. 1863-1870
SAMUEL HIDDEN WENTWORTH,
  A.M. 1870-1873
DAVID GREENE HASKINS, Jr.,
  A.M. 1873-1890
GEORGE KUHN CLARKE, LL.B. 1890-1890
GUSTAVUS ARTHUR HILTON,
  LL.B. 1890

Corresponding Secretaries.

SAMUEL GARDNER DRAKE, { 1845-1850
  A.M. . . . .(1851-1858
NATHANIEL BRADSTREET
  SHURTLEFF, M.D. 1850-1851
SAMUEL HOPKINS RIDDEL
  (Rev.), A.M. 1858-1859
JOHN WARD DEAN, A.M. . . 1859-1862
CALEB DAVIS BRADLEE, D.D. 1862-1865

HENRY MARTYN DEXTER, D.D.,
  LL.D.. 1865-1867
EDMUND FARWELL SLAFTER,
  D.D. 1867-1887
HAMILTON ANDREWS HILL,
  A.M. 1887-1889
FRANCIS HENRY BROWN, M.D. 1889-1892
HENRY HERBERT EDES . . 1892

[1] See United States.   [2] See Delaware.

ALMON DANFORTH HODGES { 1859-1861
{ 1878-1878

CHARLES HUDSON, A.M. . 1859-1861

CALEB DAVIS BRADLEE, D.D. { 1859-1867
{ 1869-1889

GEORGE WASHINGTON MES- { 1860-1861
SINGER (Hon.) . . . { 1862-1868
{ 1869-1870

WINSLOW LEWIS, M.D. . . . 1861-1875

MARTIN MOORE (Rev.), A.M. 1861-1866

WILLIAM BLANCHARD TOWNE,
A.M. 1861-1876

JOHN HANNIBAL SHEPPARD,
A.M. 1861-1873

EDWARD FRANKLIN EVERETT.
A.M. 1862-1863

WILLIAM BLAKE TRASK, A.M. 1862-1889

JEREMIAH COLBURN, A.M. . 1862-1889

WILLIAM REED DEANE. . . 1862-1871

JOSEPH PALMER, M.D. . . . 1862-1871

JOHN BARSTOW 862-1864

EDWARD SPRAGUE RAND, Jr.,
A.M. 1863-1878

HORATIO ALGER, Jr. (Rev.),
A.B. 1863-1865

HENRY MARTYN DEXTER, D.D.
LL.D. 1864-1867

WILLIAM HENRY WHITMORE,
A.M. 1864-1889

FREDERIC WEST HOLLAND
(Rev.), A.M. 1864-1867

WASHINGTON GILBERT (Rev.),
A.M. 1865-1866

JOHN ALBION ANDREW, LL.D. 1866-1867

GEORGE BRUCE UPTON (Hon.) 1866-1874

EDMUND FARWELL SLAFTER,
D.D. 1867-1889

JOHN MERRILL BRADBURY . 1867-1870

CHARLES WESLEY TUTTLE,
A.M. 1867-1881

MARSHALL PINCKNEY WILDER,
LL.D. 1868-1886

DORUS CLARKE, D.D. . . . 1868-1884

WILLIAM JAMES FOLEY . . . 1869-1871

HENRY EDWARDS . . . . { 1869-1871
{ 1876-1885

ALBERT HARRISON HOYT, A.M. 1869-1889

EDWARD SILAS TOBEY, A.M. 1870-1874

SAMUEL HIDDEN WENTWORTH,
A.M. 1870-1873

BENJAMIN BARSTOW TORREY 1871-1889

JAMES FROTHINGHAM HUNNE-
WELL, A.M. 1871-1889

SAMUEL BURNHAM, A.M. . . 1871-1872

JOHN CUMMINGS, Jr. (Hon.) . 1871-1889

JOHN FOSTER 1871-1889

DAVID GREENE HASKINS, Jr.,
A.M. 1873-1889

THOMAS COFFIN AMORY, Jr.,
A.M. 1873-1889

CHARLES LEVI WOODBURY
(Hon.) 1874-1875

SAMUEL ADAMS DRAKE . . 1874-1875

GEORGE CARTER RICHARDSON
(Hon.) 1875-1886

SAMUEL CUTLER (Rev.) . . 1875-1880

JAMES WALKER AUSTIN, A.M. 1877-1889

CYRUS WOODMAN, A.M. . . 1878-1889

JOHN GARDNER WHITE, A.M. 1878-1889

HENRY HARRISON SPRAGUE,
A.M. 1878-1879

HENRY WARE HOLLAND, LL.B. 1878-1880

NATHANIEL FOSTER SAFFORD,
A.B. 1879-1889

INCREASE NILES TARBOX,
D.D. 1881-1888

JOHN TYLER HASSAM, A.M. . 1882-1889

WILLIAM CLAFLIN, LL.D. . . 1883-1889

ALVAH AUGUSTUS BURRAGE
(Hon.). 1884-1889

HENRY ALLEN HAZEN, D.D. . 1884-1889

ABNER CHENEY GOODELL, Jr.
A.M. 1884-1889

WILLIAM GORDON MEANS. . 1884-1889

GEORGE HENRY PREBLE,
U.S.N. 1885-1885

CHARLES LOUIS FLINT, A.M. 1885-1889

JOHN FORRESTER ANDREW,
A.M. 1886-1888

JOHN JOSEPH MAY 1887-1889

HAMILTON ANDREWS HILL,
A.M. 1887-1889

WILLARD SPENCER ALLEN,
A.M. 1888-1889

JOHN COFFIN JONES BROWN . 1888-1889

CHARLES DEANE, LL.D. . . 1851–1851	WILLIAM BLANCHARD TOWNE,
TIMOTHY FARRAR, LL.D. . . {1851–1854, 1857–1858}	A.M. 1865–1876
FREDERIC KIDDER . . . {1851–1855, 1867–1868}	ALBERT HARRISON HOYT, {1867–1877, A.M. 1889–1891}
WILLIAM BLAKE TRASK, A.M. {1852–1853, 1858–1867, 1876–1889}	CHARLES WESLEY TUTTLE, A.M. 1872–1873
CHARLES MAYO 1852–1853	GEORGE HENRY PREBLE, U.S.N. 1872–1874
WILLIAM JENKS, D.D., LL.D. . 1853–1858	HENRY HERBERT EDES . . {1873–1876, 1877}
LYMAN MASON, A.M. . . . 1853–1854	JEREMIAH COLBURN, A.M. . . 1874–1889
JOHN WARD DEAN, A.M. . . 1854–1889	HENRY FITZGILBERT WATERS,
WILLIAM REED DEANE . . . 1854–1856	A.M. 1877–1883
ALONZO HALL QUINT, D.D. . 1855–1856	EDMUND FARWELL SLAFTER,
JAMES SPEAR LORING . . . 1855–1856	D.D. 1879–1889
FRANCIS BRINLEY, A.M. . . 1856–1858	HENRY EDWARD WAITE . . 1885–1889
CHARLES HENRY MORSE . . 1856–1858	FRANCIS EVERETT BLAKE . . 1885–1889
WILLIAM HENRY WHITMORE, {1856–1861, A.M. 1862–1872}	FRANCIS HENRY BROWN, M.D. 1889
CHARLES HUDSON, A.M. . . 1861–1863	JOHN TYLER HASSAM, A.M. . 1889–1891
ELIAS NASON (Rev.), A.M. . . {1861–1864, 1865–1868}	FRANK ELIOT BRADISH, A.B. 1889–1891
GEORGE WINGATE CHASE . . 1861–1862	HENRY FITCH JENKS (Rev.), A.M. 1891
WILLIAM SUMNER APPLETON, A.M. 1863–1872	EGBERT COFFIN SMYTH, D.D. 1891–1891
HENRY MARTYN DEXTER, D.D., LL.D. 1864–1867	ANDREW McFARLAND DAVIS, S.B. 1891
	BENJAMIN APTHORP GOULD, LL.D. 1891

Editors of the Register.

The two volumes issued in 1859 and 1860 were edited by Messrs. Trask, Whitmore, and Dean jointly. An account of the *New-England Historical and Genealogical Register* from 1847 to 1876 will be found in the Society's *Proceedings* for January, 1876, pp. 42–48.

WILLIAM COGSWELL, D.D.	January, 1847–October, 1847.
SAMUEL GARDNER DRAKE, A.M.	January, 1848–January, 1849.
	January, 1850.
	January, 1851–October, 1851.
	January, 1853–October, 1858.
	January, 1861–October, 1861.
WILLIAM THADDEUS HARRIS, A.M.	April, 1849–October, 1849.
NATHANIEL BRADSTREET SHURTLEFF, M.D.	April, 1850–October, 1850.
JOSEPH BARLOW FELT (Rev.), LL.D.	January, 1852–April, 1852.
TIMOTHY FARRAR, LL.D.	July, 1852.
WILLIAM BLAKE TRASK, A.M.	October, 1852.
	January, 1859–October, 1860.
	January, 1862.
	January, 1864–April, 1864.
	January, 1865–October, 1865.
WILLIAM HENRY WHITMORE, A.M.	January, 1859–October, 1860.

JOHN WARD DEAN, A.M.	January, 1859–October, 1860.
	October, 1862–October, 1863.
	July, 1864–October, 1864.
	January, 1876–January, 1889.
ELIAS NASON (Rev.), A.M.	April, 1862.
	January, 1866–October, 1867.
CHARLES HUDSON, A.M.	July, 1862.
ALBERT HARRISON HOYT, A.M..	January, 1868–October, 1875.

---·---

Register Club.

The Register Club was formed in the summer of 1864 to secure the continuance of the Quarterly. The members pledged themselves to bear the responsibility of its publication, which was assumed by the Society upon the dissolution of the Club in the autumn of 1874. — *Proceedings*, January, 1876, p. 44.

WINSLOW LEWIS, M.D.	1865, 1866, 1869, 1871
WILLIAM BLANCHARD TOWNE, A.M.	1865–1874.
FREDERIC KIDDER	1865–1874.
CHARLES SUMNER FELLOWS	1865–1870.
WILLIAM BLAKE TRASK, A.M.	1865–1874.
WILLIAM HENRY WHITMORE, A.M..	1865, 1866, 1868, 1869.
WILLIAM SUMNER APPLETON, A.M..	1865, 1868, 1870.
SAMUEL GARDNER DRAKE, A.M.	1865–1870, 1872.
JOHN KIMBALL WIGGIN	1865–1868.
JOHN WARD DEAN, A.M..	1865–1874.
JEREMIAH COLBURN, A.M.	1865–1874.
JOHN MERRILL BRADBURY	1865–1868.
DELORAINE PENDRE COREY	1865–1874.
EDWARD SPRAGUE RAND, Jr., A.M.	1865, 1866, 1868.
GEORGE WASHINGTON MESSINGER (Hon.)	1865.
ALONZO HALL QUINT, D.D.	1865, 1866, 1870.
CALVIN FLETCHER, A.M..	1865, 1866.
ALMON DANFORTH HODGES.	1865.
DAVID CLAPP	1865.
HENRY MARTYN DEXTER, D.D.	1865.
CHARLES WESLEY TUTTLE. A.M.	1866–1874.
EBENEZER WEAVER PEIRCE	1866.
WILLIAM REED DEANE	1866–1869.
FRANCIS FRENCH	1866.
EDMUND FARWELL SLAFTER, D.D.	1867–1872, 1874.
ELIAS NASON (Rev.), A.M.	1868.
ALBERT HARRISON HOYT, A.M.	1868–1874.
MARSHALL PINCKNEY WILDER, LL.D.	1868–1874.
HENRY HERBERT EDES	1870–1874.
DORUS CLARKE, D.D.	1871–1873.
THOMAS WATERMAN	1871, 1872.
GEORGE HENRY PREBLE, U.S.N.	1871–1874.
JOHN HANNIBAL SHEPPARD, A.M.	1872, 1873.
LUCIUS ROBINSON PAIGE, D.D.	1874.

CONTENTS.

ROLLS OF MEMBERSHIP.

List of Resident Members.

FOUNDERS.

17 December, 1844.

NAME.	RESIDENCE.	MEMBERSHIP CEASED.
CHARLES EWER	Boston . . .	Died 12 November, 1853.
LEMUEL SHATTUCK	Boston . . .	Died 17 January, 1859.
SAMUEL GARDNER DRAKE, A.M. .	Boston . . .	Elected Honorary Member, 4 January, 1860.
WILLIAM HENRY MONTAGUE . .	Boston . . .	Died 15 May, 1889.
JOHN WINGATE THORNTON, A.M., LL. B.	Boston . . .	Life Member, 1863. Died 6 June, 1878.

MEMBERS ELECTED.

21 January, 1845.

LUCIUS ROBINSON PAIGE, A.M , D.D. Cambridge.

FREDERIC PALMER TRACY (Rev.) . Williamsburgh Resigned 6 January, 1846. Elected Corresponding Member, 2 December, 1857.

SAMUEL HOPKINS RIDDEL (Rev.), A.M. Boston . . . Died 1 June, 1876.

JOSEPH WILLARD, A.M., LL.B. . Boston . . . Died 12 May, 1865.

6 February, 1845.

NAHUM MITCHELL, A.M. . . . . . Boston . . . Elected Corresponding Member. 7 May, 1845.

RICHARD FROTHINGHAM, Jr., A.M., LL.D. Charlestown . Died 29 January, 1880.

1

NAME.	RESIDENCE.	MEMBERSHIP CEASED.
WILLIAM INGALLS, A.M., M.B., M.D.	Boston . . .	Died 9 September, 1851.
JONATHAN MASON	Boston . . .	Resigned 7 January, 1852. Re-elected 3 May, 1871.
CHANDLER ROBBINS, A.M., D.D. .	Boston . . .	Resigned 1 January, 1851.
NATHANIEL BRADSTREET SHURTLEFF, A.M., M.D.	Boston . . .	Died 17 October, 1874.
JAMES SPEAR LORING	Boston . .	Elected Corresponding Member, 3 November, 1858.

20 February, 1845.

CHARLES DEANE, A.M., LL.D.. .	Boston . . .	Died 13 November, 1889.

25 February, 1845.

WILLIAM WHITWELL GREENOUGH, A.B.	Boston . . .	Life Member, 1863.
EDWARD TUCKERMAN, A.M., LL.B., LL.D.	Cambridge .	Resigned 1859.
JAMES MURRAY ROBBINS	Boston . . .	Resigned 1 January, 1851.
ANDREW HENSHAW WARD, A.M. .	Newton . .	Died 18 February, 1864.

7 March, 1845.

HORATIO GATES SOMERBY . . .	Boston . .	Elected Corresponding Member, 3 August, 1859.

20 March, 1845.

THOMAS BULFINCH, A.M. . . .	Boston . . .	Resigned 5 January, 1848.
DAVID REED, A.M.	Boston . . .	Resgd. 5 November, 1851.
WILLIAM JOSEPH ADAMS, A.M. .	Boston . . .	Resigned 6 January, 1847.

1 April, 1845.

WILLIAM REED DEANE . . .	Boston . . .	Life Member, 1863. Died 16 June, 1871.
GEORGE WINSLOW	Boston . . .	Resgd. 19 February, 1850.

15 April, 1845.

SAMUEL TURELL ARMSTRONG . .	Boston . . .	Died 26 March, 1850.
BENJAMIN VINTON FRENCH . . .	Braintree . .	Life Member, 1857. Died 11 April, 1860.
WILLIAM HYSLOP SUMNER, A.M. .	Boston . . .	Died 24 October, 1861.
JOHN HENSHAW	Boston . . .	Resigned 6 January, 1847.

7 May, 1845.

NAME.	RESIDENCE.	MEMBERSHIP CEASED.
JOHN GORHAM PALFREY, A.M., D.D., LL.D.	Boston . . .	Resigned 2 January, 1850.
CHARLES HARRISON STEDMAN, A.M., M.D.	Boston . . .	Resigned 3 January, 1849.

4 June, 1845.

THOMAS WHITTEMORE, D.D. . .	Cambridge .	Resigned 5 January, 1853.
FREDERIC TURELL GRAY (Rev.), A.M.	Boston . . .	Died 9 March, 1855.

18 June, 1845.

WILLIAM PITT GREENWOOD, D.D.S.	Boston . . .	Died 10 May, 1851.
WILLIAM POWELL MASON, A.M. .	Boston . . .	Died 4 December, 1867.
SOLOMON LINCOLN, A.M.	Hingham . .	Life Member, 1871. Died 1 December, 1881.
ABNER PHELPS, M.D.	Boston . . .	Resigned 6 January, 1846.

1 July, 1845.

FRANCIS NALDER MITCHELL . .	Boston . . .	Resigned 3 January, 1855.

6 August, 1845.

ADOLPHUS DAVIS	Boston . . .	5 April, 1870.
WILLIAM THADDEUS HARRIS, A.M., LL.B.	Cambridge .	Died 19 October, 1854.
DAVID HAMBLEN	Boston . . .	Died 29 November, 1855.

3 September, 1845.

EDMUND BATCHELDER DEARBORN .	Boston . . .	Life Member, 1858. Died 22 January, 1886.
WALDO HIGGINSON, A.M. .	Boston . . .	Resigned 5 January, 1853. Re-elected 4 April, 1883.

4 November, 1845.

WILLIAM HENRY KELLEY . . .	Boston . . .	Resgd. 2 February, 1858. Elected Corresponding Member, 2 June, 1858.

6 January, 1846.

EDWARD EVERETT, A.M., Ph.D., D.C.L., LL.D.	Boston . . .	Died 15 January, 1865.
CALEB BATES	Hingham . .	Died 16 September, 1857.

4 February, 1846.

NAME.	RESIDENCE.	MEMBERSHIP CEASED.
WILLIAM IVES BUDINGTON, A.M., D.D.	Charlestown	Elected Corresponding Member, 13 December, 1848.
NATHANIEL WHEELER COFFIN	Boston	Died 26 August, 1869.

7 April, 1846.

THOMAS CARTER SMITH	Boston	Died 24 September, 1880.

3 June, 1846.

JOSIAH FLAGG LEACH	Boston	Resigned 2 January, 1850.
JOHN HARRISON BLAKE	Boston	Resigned 9 March, 1876.
ISAAC CHILD	Boston	Life Member, 1860. Died 23 December, 1885.

7 July, 1846.

SAMUEL SWETT, A.M.	Boston	Died 28 October, 1866.
GARLAND TURELL	Boston	Resigned 7 January, 1852.

5 August, 1846.

WILLIAM TURELL ANDREWS, A.M.	Boston	Resigned 7 January, 1852. Re-elected 6 April, 1870.
CALEB EDDY	Boston	Resgd. 10 February, 1849.
EDWARD EVERETT HALE, A.M., D.D.	Worcester	Resigned 1 January, 1851. Re-elected 3 June, 1891. Fees commuted, 1891.

7 October, 1846.

JARED SPARKS, A.M., LL.D.	Cambridge	Died 4 March, 1866.
SAMUEL ATKINS ELIOT, A.M.	Boston	Resgd. 19 February, 1850.
THEODORE LYMAN, Jr., A.M.	Boston	Died 18 July, 1849.
HORATIO NELSON OTIS	New York, N.Y.	Resigned 3 January, 1849.
EDWARD FULLER HODGES, A.B.	Boston	Resigned 2 January, 1850.
ABBOTT LAWRENCE, LL.D.	Boston	Died 18 August, 1855.
GEORGE LIVERMORE, A.M.	Cambridge	Resigned 1 January, 1851.

4 November, 1846.

JOSEPH WARREN WRIGHT	Boston	Resigned 26 January, 1869.

6 January, 1847.

DANIEL PINCKNEY PARKER	Boston	Elected Honorary Member, 3 March, 1847.

NAME.	RESIDENCE.	MEMBERSHIP CEASED.
FREDERIC WALKER LINCOLN, Jr., A. M.	Boston . . .	Life Member, 1863.
CHARLES MAYO ELLIS, A. B. . .	Roxbury . .	Resigned 3 January, 1849.

3 March. 1847.

MARTIN MOORE (Rev.). A. M. . .	Boston . . .	Died 11 March, 1866.
THOMAS LARKIN TURNER	Boston.	
WILLIAM THOMAS GREEN MORTON, M. D.	Boston . . .	2 August, 1851.

7 April, 1847.

WILLIAM SAVAGE	Boston . . .	Died 30 June, 1851.
STEPHEN PALMER FULLER . . .	Boston . . .	Resigned 3 January, 1849.
CHARLES STODDARD	Boston . . .	Resigned 4 February, 1852.
NATHANIEL MORTON DAVIS, A. M.	Plymouth . .	Died 29 July, 1848.
RALPH HASKINS	Roxbury . .	Died 9 November, 1852.
HARRISON GRAY OTIS COLBY, A. M.	New Bedford.	Died 21 February, 1853.
WILLIAM THOMAS	Boston . . .	Resigned 3 January, 1849. Re-elected 3 March, 1869.
ROBERT CHARLES WINTHROP, A. M., LL. D.	Boston . . .	Life Member, 1872.

5 May. 1847.

SIMON GREENLEAF, A. M., LL.D. .	Boston . . .	Died 6 October, 1853.
WILLIAM HAYDEN	Boston . . .	Resigned 2 January, 1872.
GEORGE BRUCE UPTON	Boston . . .	Life Member, 1863. Died 1 July, 1874.
ENOCH TRAIN	Boston . . .	Resigned 16 July, 1855.
STEPHEN MINOT WELD, A. M. . .	Roxbury . .	Died 13 December, 1867.
ALBERT FEARING	Boston . . .	Resigned 6 January, 1863. Re-elected 3 March, 1869.
ANDREW BIGELOW, A. M., D. D. .	Boston . . .	Resigned 2 January, 1850.

2 June, 1847.

ALEXANDER WILSON MCCLURE, A. M., D. D.	Boston . . .	Resigned 5 January, 1853.
DAVID PULSIFER, A. M.	Boston.	
WILLIAM PARSONS	Boston . . .	See Corresponding Roll, 5 May, 1847. Life Member, 1870. Died 1 July, 1885.
CHARLES COTESWORTH PINCKNEY MOODY.	Boston . . .	Resigned 4 January, 1854.

NAME.	RESIDENCE.	MEMBERSHIP CEASED.
JOSEPH BARLOW FELT (Rev.), A.M., LL.D.	Boston . . .	See Corresponding Roll, 20 March, 1845. Elected Honorary Member 3 October, 1855.

7 July, 1847.

JOSHUA HUNTINGTON WOLCOTT	. Boston . . .	Life Member, 1872. Died 4 January, 1891.

4 August, 1847.

THEODORE LYMAN HOWE . . .	Boston . .	Resigned 8 February, 1849.
HORATIO HOLLIS HUNNEWELL . .	Boston . . .	Resigned 7 January, 1852. Re-elected 4 May, 1870.
BENJAMIN PARKER RICHARDSON .	Boston . . .	Died 17 November, 1870.

1 September, 1847.

CHARLES JAMES FOX BINNEY . .	Boston . . .	Resigned 5 January, 1853.

7 October, 1847.

AMOS ADAMS LAWRENCE, A.M. .	Boston . . .	Life Member, 1863. Died 22 August, 1886.

3 November, 1847.

WILLIAM SUTTON	Salem . . .	Life Member, 1871. Died 18 April, 1882.

5 January, 1848.

ELIAS NASON (Rev.), A.M. . . .	Newburyport .	See Corresponding Roll, 3 March, 1847. Life Member, 1867. Died 17 June, 1887.
BARON STOW, A.M., D.D. . . .	Boston . . .	Resgd. 31 December, 1853.
DANIEL GILBERT	Boston . . .	Died 4 August, 1849.
ANDREW JOHONNOT	Boston . . .	Died 20 August, 1860.

2 February, 1848.

ISRAEL PUTNAM PROCTOR . . .	Boston . . .	Died 16 October, 1851.

1 March, 1848.

THOMAS HOOKER LEAVITT . . .	Boston . . .	Resgd. 27 February, 1877.
ARTEMAS SIMONDS	Boston . . .	Died 15 October, 1854.
GEORGE WASHINGTON MESSINGER	Boston . . .	Life Member, 1860. Died 27 April, 1870.

5 April, 1848.

PLINY NICKERSON	Boston . . .	Resigned 7 January, 1852.

3 May, 1848.

Name.	Residence.	Membership ceased.
CHARLES MAYO	Boston . .	Died 2 January, 1859.
SAMUEL ANDREWS . . .	Boston . .	Resgd. 13 December, 1862.

4 October, 1848.

JUSTIN WINSOR, A. B., LL. D. . . Boston . . . Resigned 7 January, 1852.

11 July, 1849.

FREDERIC KIDDER . . . . . . Boston . .	Life Member, 1863. Died 19 December, 1885.
HENRY HOLTON FULLER, A. M. . Boston . . .	Died 15 September, 1852.
NATHANIEL HAMLEN . . . . . Boston . . .	Resigned 7 January, 1852.

10 January, 1850.

THOMAS BELLOWS WYMAN, Jr. . . . Charlestown . See Corresponding Roll, 2 December, 1846. Life Member, 1858. Died 19 May, 1878.

6 February, 1850.

BENJAMIN HOMER DIXON . .	Boston . . .	Resgd. 12 December, 1857. Elected Corresponding Member, 5 August, 1863.
SAMUEL HAYNES JENKS	Boston . . .	Resigned 3 January, 1855.
TIMOTHY FARRAR, A.M., LL. D.	Boston . . .	Elected Honorary Member, 3 August, 1859.
HENRY DAVENPORT	Roxbury . .	Life Member, 1873.
JOHN GOODWIN LOCKE	Boston . . .	Died 22 July, 1869.
ELEAZER FRANKLIN PRATT . . .	Boston . . .	Died 14 October, 1888.
JOHN DEAN.[1] A.M.	Boston . . .	Life Member, 1859.
ISAAC WINSLOW	Boston . .	2 March, 1869.

6 March, 1850.

ELISHA FULLER, A.M. . . . . . Worcester. .	Died 18 March, 1855.
JOSEPH MOULTON . . . . . . Lynn . . .	Died 10 February, 1873.

1 May, 1850.

MARSHALL PINCKNEY WILDER, Ph.D., LL.D.	Dorchester	Life Member, 1863. Died 16 December, 1886.
WILLIAM MATTHEW WALLACE . . Boston . . .		Resigned 1 January, 1856.

3 July, 1850.

SAMUEL JAMES BRIDGE, A.M. . . Boston . . .	Resigned 5 January, 1853. Re-elected 4 November, 1874.
ALONZO HALL QUINT, A.M., D.D. Andover . .	Life Member, 1861.

[1] Mr. Dean changed his name to John Ward Dean in 1857.

7 November, 1850.

NAME.	RESIDENCE.	MEMBERSHIP CEASED.
WILLIAM WADE COWLES	Boston . . .	Resigned 5 January, 1853. Re-elected 2 March, 1864.
FREDERICK WILLIAM PRESCOTT .	Boston . . .	Resgd. 23 February, 1870.

5 December, 1850.

WILLIAM LOCKE BROWN	South Reading	Resigned 30 June, 1857.
JONATHAN BROWN BRIGHT . . .	Waltham . .	Life Member, 1863. Died 17 December, 1879.

18 December, 1850.

CHARLES GREELY LORING, A. M., LL. D.	Boston . . .	Died 8 October, 1867.
LUCIUS MANLIUS SARGENT, A. M. .	Boston . . .	Died 2 June, 1867.
GEORGE HINCKLEY LYMAN, M. D. .	Boston . . .	Resgd. 9 December, 1859.

5 February, 1851.

HENRY CHARDON BROOKS . . .	Boston . . .	5 April, 1859.
SYLVESTER BLISS	Boston . . .	Resgd. 27 December, 1861.
JACOB QUINCY KETTELLE, A. B. .	Boston . . .	Died 2 December, 1865.
JOHN WELLS PARKER	Roxbury . .	Life Member, 1871. Died 3 June, 1875.
GUY CARLETON HAYNES	Boston . . .	Resgd. 13 December, 1861.
AMASA WALKER, LL. D.	Boston . . .	Resigned 4 January, 1854. Re-elected 3 November, 1869.
FRANCIS BRINLEY, A. M.	Boston . . .	Resigned 1 January, 1859.

5 March, 1851.

JOHN ISRAEL BAKER	Beverly . .	Life Member, 1863.
JOHN RODMAN ROLLINS, A. M. . .	Boston . . .	Life Member, 1872.
DANIEL CLEMENT COLESWORTHY .	Boston . . .	Resgd. 4 December, 1861.
WILLIAM GRAY BROOKS	Boston . . .	Died 6 January, 1879.

7 May, 1851.

WILLIAM LINCOLN	Boston . . .	Resgd. 2 September, 1856.

4 June, 1851.

HENRY BLATCHFORD WHEELWRIGHT, A. M.	Taunton . .	Resigned 4 January, 1854.
ISAAC DAVIS, A. M., LL. D. . . .	Worcester . .	5 April, 1859.
JOHN DOANE, Jr.	Charlestown .	Resigned 2 January, 1853.

6 August, 1851.

NAME.	RESIDENCE.	MEMBERSHIP CEASED.
WILLIAM BLAKE TRASK, A. M.	Dorchester	Life Member, 1858.

3 September, 1851.

WILLIAM SCUDDER THACHER	Boston	Resgd. 17 December, 1862.

1 October, 1851.

ADDISON CHILD	Medford	Life Member, 1870.
ALFRED POOR [1]	Bradford	Life Member, 1873.

5 November, 1851.

LUTHER METCALF HARRIS, A.M., M.D.	West Roxbury	Died 28 January, 1865.

3 December, 1851.

SAMUEL JENNISON, A. M.	Worcester	Died 11 March. 1860.

7 January, 1852.

WILLIAM WHITING, A.M., LL. B., LL. D.	Roxbury	Life Member. 1871. Died 29 June. 1873.
THOMAS PRINCE	Boston	Resigned January, 1870.

4 February, 1852.

THOMAS WATERMAN	Boston	Died 27 February, 1875.
JOSEPH PALMER. A.M., M.D.	Boston	Died 3 March, 1871.

3 March, 1852.

HENRY HALL JONES	Boston	Resgd. 1 February, 1859.
STEPHEN THURSTON FARWELL	Cambridge	Died 20 October, 1872.
MOSES PLIMPTON	Boston	Died 19 September, 1854.

5 May, 1852.

GEORGE ADAMS	Boston	Died 4 October, 1865.
HENRY BRIGHT	Northampton	Resigned 14 March, 1861.

3 June, 1852.

RICHARD PITTS	Dorchester	Resigned 3 January, 1855.

[1] Mr. Poor now (1892) writes his name " Poore."

7 July, 1852.

NAME.	RESIDENCE.	MEMBERSHIP CEASED.
EBEN SPERRY STEARNS, A.M., D. D., LL. D.	Newton	Resigned 5 January, 1853. Elected Corresponding Member, 2 March, 1859.
WILLIAM HENRY CHASE, U. S. A.	Pensacola, Fla.	2 March, 1869.

1 September, 1852.

AMOS BRONSON ALCOTT	Boston	Resigned 1 January, 1862.
CHARLES SPRAGUE LINCOLN, A.B.	Somerville	Resigned 5 January, 1853.
CHARLES ADAMS, JR., A.M.	Boston	Died 19 April, 1886.
WILLIAM BLANCHARD TOWNE, A.M.	Brookline	Life Member, 1860. Died 10 April, 1876.

3 November, 1852.

ALMON DANFORTH HODGES	Roxbury	Life Member, 1859. Died 27 September, 1878.
LYMAN MASON, A.M.	Boston.	
JOHN GEORGE METCALF, A. M., M. D.	Mendon	Died 12 January, 1892.
JOHN PLUMMER HEALY, A.M., LL.D.	Boston	Life Member, 1873. Died 4 January, 1882.

1 December, 1852.

ALEXANDER LEBARON MONROE, M.D.	Medway	31 December, 1863.

2 February, 1853.

GEORGE MATHER CHAMPNEY	Woburn	Resigned 3 January, 1855.
BOWEN BUCKMAN	Woburn	Died 23 November, 1864.
EDMUND BOYNTON	Boston	Resgd. 17 December, 1862.
DANIEL DRAPER	Boston	Died 1 June, 1867.
JOSEPH WALTER WARD	Boston	Resigned 3 January, 1855.
PAUL WILLARD, JR., A.M.	Charlestown	Died 15 August, 1868.
FREDERICK AUGUSTUS WHITNEY (Rev.), A.M.	Brighton	Life Member, 1870. Died 21 October, 1880.
ARNOLD WILLIAM CONANT	Boston	Resgd. 2 December, 1856.
WILLIAM JONES	Boston	Resigned 2 July, 1856.
SAMUEL NICOLSON	Boston	Resigned January, 1860.
SAMUEL GREENE WHEELER, JR.	Concord	5 April, 1870.

2 March, 1853.

ROGER NEWTON PIERCE	Boston	Resignation accepted 2 December, 1856.
IRA BALLOU PECK	Woonsocket, R.I.	Life Member, 1873. Died 29 June, 1888.

NAME.	RESIDENCE.	MEMBERSHIP CEASED.
CHARLES AUGUSTUS RANLETT . .	Charlestown .	Died 17 April, 1878.
HIRAM WELLINGTON, A.M., LL.B.	Boston . . .	31 December, 1880.
PETER SLUMAN WHEELOCK . .	Boston . . .	Resigned 4 January, 1854.
NATHANIEL WHITING	Charlestown .	Life Member, 1868. Died 18 November, 1871.
CHRISTOPHER COLUMBUS ANDREWS	Newton . .	Resigned 4 January, 1854.
ITHAMAR WARREN BEARD . . .	Lowell . .	Resigned 7 April, 1860.
JOHN HASKINS	Roxbury .	Resigned 4 January, 1854.
STEPHEN MERRILL ALLEN, A.M., LL.B.	Boston . .	Life Member, 1872.
BICKFORD PULSIFER, Jr.	Cambridge .	Life Member, 1873. Died 20 February, 1880.
JOSIAH DUNHAM, Jr.	Boston . . .	Life Member, 1870. Died 17 April, 1877.
DANIEL MONTGOMERY HUCKINS .	Boston . . .	Resigned 16 July, 1855.

6 April, 1853.

NATHAN APPLETON, A.M., LL.D. .	Boston . . .	See Honorary Roll, 6 January, 1847. Died 14 July, 1861.
MANNING LEONARD.	Southbridge .	Life Member, 1864. Died 31 July, 1885.
JOHN STETSON BARRY	Hanover . .	Resigned January, 1860.
JOHN MERRILL BRADBURY . . .	Boston . .	Life Member, 1863. Died 21 March, 1876.
WILLIAM DAVIS TICKNOR . .	Boston . . .	Died 10 April, 1864.
JOSIAH NEWHALL	Lynnfield . .	Life Member, 1871. Died 26 December, 1879.

1 June, 1853.

SAMUEL HENRY GILBERT, LL.B. .	Gagetown, N.B.	Resigned 4 January, 1854.
THOMAS HOPKINSON, A.M. . . .	Boston . . .	Resgd. 31 December, 1855.
BENJAMIN FRANKLIN WHITE . .	Boston . . .	Resigned 1 January, 1859.

7 September, 1853.

CHARLES FREDERICK ADAMS. JR., A.M., LL.B.	Boston . . .	Died 30 December, 1856.
ELIAS SILL HAWLEY, A.B. . . .	Buffalo, N.Y.	
JAMES MORSS CHASE, A.M., LL.B.	Cambridge .	Resigned 4 January, 1854.

5 October, 1853.

HENRY CLARK	Poultney, Vt..	Resigned 7 January, 1873.

3 November, 1853.

NAME.	RESIDENCE.	MEMBERSHIP CEASED.
LUTHER FARNHAM (Rev.), A.M.	Boston . . .	Resigned 1 April, 1861. Re-elected 3 December, 1879.
LLOYD GLOVER	Boston . . .	Died 2 August, 1862.
CHARLES HAZEN PEASLEE, A.M.	Boston . . .	Died 20 September, 1866.

7 December, 1853.

JOHN ROGERS KIMBALL	Boston . . .	Life Member, 1863. Died 17 September, 1883.

4 January, 1854.

ALONZO BOWEN CHAPIN, D.D. . .	South Glaston-bury, Conn.	Resignation accepted 3 February, 1857.
CHARLES ATWOOD, A.M.	Boston . . .	Resgd. 15 November, 1867.

1 February, 1854.

OLIVER CARTER	Boston . . .	Resigned 31 January, 1860.
STEPHEN CARVER SIMMONS . . .	Boston . . .	5 September, 1865.
DANIEL NOYES HASKELL	Boston . . .	Died 14 November, 1874.
WILLIAM HENRY WHITMORE, A.M.	Boston.	

1 March, 1854.

THOMAS SCOTT PEARSON, A.M.	Peacham, Vt..	Died 10 November, 1856.
JOHN WRIGHT WARREN, M.D. . .	Boston . . .	Life Member, 1863. Died 4 January, 1869.

3 May, 1854.

GORHAM BROOKS, A.M.	Medford . .	Died 10 September, 1855.
SAMUEL HALL	East Boston .	Died 13 November, 1870.

6 September, 1854.

WILLIAM STOODLEY BARTLET (Rev.), A.M.	Chelsea	Resigned 14 July, 1875.

4 October, 1854.

DEAN DUDLEY	Boston . . .	31 December, 1880.

6 December, 1854.

HERMAN POWERS	Boston . .	Resgd. 22 December, 1868.
URIEL CROCKER, A.M.	Boston . . .	Died 19 July, 1887.
TOLMAN WILLEY	Boston . . .	31 December, 1866.
LEMUEL LITTLE	Boston . . .	Died 15 March, 1878.

3 January, 1855.

NAME.	RESIDENCE.	MEMBERSHIP CEASED.
WILLIAM SAXTON MORTON, A. M.	Quincy . . .	Life Member, 1871. Died 21 September, 1871.
ALEXANDER BLAIKIE (Rev.) . .	Boston . .	Resgd. 24 November, 1863.

7 February, 1855.

SAMUEL SMITH KILBURN, Jr. . .	Newton.	
CHARLES HENRY MORSE . . .	Boston . . .	5 April, 1870.
JOHN ALONZO BOUTELLE . . .	Woburn	Died 15 December, 1880.
THOMAS JEFFERSON WHITTEMORE	Cambridge . .	2 March, 1869.

7 March, 1855.

JEREMIAH PEABODY JEWETT, M. D.	Lowell . . .	Died 23 June, 1870.
AMOS OTIS	Yarmouth . .	See Corresponding Roll, 7 July. 1847. Died 19 October. 1875.
JOSEPH ALLEN, A. M., D. D. . .	Northborough .	Died 23 February, 1873.

4 April, 1855.

GEORGE LUNT, A. B.	Boston . . .	See Corresponding Roll, 5 May, 1847. Resgd. 23 January, 1874.
WILLIAM JOSEPH REYNOLDS . .	Boston . . .	Resgd. 16 December, 1861.
ALEXANDER BEAL	Boston . . .	Life Member, 1871. Died 25 January, 1890.

6 June, 1855.

FRANKLIN HAVEN, A. M. . . .	Boston . . .	Life Member, 1870.
LABAN MOREY WHEATON,[1] A. M. .	Norton . . .	Died 17 January, 1865.

11 July, 1855.

CHARLES COFFIN JEWETT, A. M. .	Washington, D.C.	Died 9 January, 1868.
THOMAS EUGENE GRAVES . . .	Thompson, Conn.	5 April, 1859.
GEORGE GIRDLER SMITH . . .	Boston . . .	Died 18 December, 1878.
JAMES WILSON CLARK	Framingham .	Life Member, 1870.

1 August, 1855.

ISAAC PARKER, A. M.	Boston . .	Died 27 May, 1858.
PHILIP HOWES SEARS, A. M., LL. B.	Boston.	
CHARLES HENRY BROMEDGE CALD-WELL. U.S.N.	Jamaica Plain .	Resigned 2 January, 1867.

[1] Cf. Clarke's *History of Norton*, p. 496; and REGISTER, XX, 85; with Brown University Triennial (1817), which gives *Mitchell* as his middle name.

5 September, 1855.

NAME.	RESIDENCE.	MEMBERSHIP CEASED.
ISRAEL THORNDIKE	New York, N.Y.	Died 8 March, 1867.
GEORGE QUINCY THORNDIKE, A.M.	New York, N.Y.	Life Member, 1870. Died 27 December, 1886.
HENRY RICE	Boston . . .	Died 15 October, 1867.
AARON SARGENT, Jr.	Somerville.	
HORATIO NELSON BIGELOW . . .	Clinton . . .	Resigned 3 October, 1862.

3 October, 1855.

CHARLES KNAPP DILLAWAY, A.M.	Roxbury . .	Resigned 17 April, 1859.
WILLIAM McCRACKAN LATHROP, A.M.	Boston . . .	Life Member, 1870. Died 24 August, 1876.
EPHRAIM GROVES WARE	Boston . . .	Died 8 November, 1862.
RICHARD KELLOGG SWIFT . . .	Chicago, Ill. .	Resignation accepted 4 September, 1860.

7 November, 1855.

THOMAS COFFIN AMORY, Jr., A.M.	Boston . . .	Died 20 August, 1889.

5 December, 1855.

LEWIS HENRY WEBB	Rockingham, N.C.	5 April, 1870.
GEORGE DANA BOARDMAN BLAN-CHARD	Malden . .	Life Member, 1863.
ALVAH AUGUSTUS BURRAGE . .	Boston . . .	Life Member, 1863.
CHARLES HUDSON, A.M. . . .	Lexington . .	Died 4 May, 1881.

2 January, 1856.

ANDREW FERDINANDO WARNER .	Cromwell, Conn.	Died 26 July, 1856.
JAMES DIMAN GREEN (Rev.), A.M.	Cambridge . .	Died 18 August, 1882.
SAMUEL BRADLEY NOYES, A.M. .	Canton . . .	Life Member, 1870.
SAMUEL HOOPER, A.M.	Boston . . .	Life Member, 1871. Died 14 February, 1875.

6 February, 1856.

HENRY AUSTIN WHITNEY, A.M. .	Boston . . .	Life Member, 1863. Died 21 February, 1889.
WILLIAM MAKEPEACE	Boston . . .	Died 26 March, 1881.
WILLIAM MASON CORNELL, A.M., M.D., D.D., LL.D.	Boston . . .	See 1 December, 1869. Elected Corresponding Member, 2 November, 1859.

5 March, 1856.

Name.	Residence.	Membership ceased.
Francis De Witt	Ware	Resgd. 23 December, 1861.
James Howard Means, A.M., D.D.	Dorchester	Life Member, 1867.

2 April, 1856.

Samuel Lane Wheeler	Newton	Resigned 4 January, 1871.
Calvin Ellis Stowe, A.M., D.D.	Andover	Resgd. 22 December, 1874.

7 May, 1856.

William Henry Leland Smith, A.B., LL.B.	Boston	Resigned 24 May, 1862.
Caleb Davis Bradlee, A.M., Ph.D., D.D.	Cambridge	Life Member, 1867.

4 June, 1856.

William Phillips, A.B.	Boston	Resigned 26 April, 1861.
Gardner Braman Perry, A.M., D.D.	Groveland	Died 16 December, 1859.

6 August, 1856.

Leverett Saltonstall, A.M., LL.B.	Newton.	
Charles Benjamin Richardson	Boston	Elected Corresponding Member, 3 November, 1858.
Abijah Weld Draper, M.D.	West Roxbury	Died 19 March, 1874.
Day Otis Kellogg	Brooklyn, N.Y.	Died 9 August, 1874.
William Low Weston	Danvers	Resgd. 25 October, 1871. Re-elected 6 January, 1875.
Jacob Whittemore Reed	Groveland	Died 10 November, 1869.

3 September, 1856.

Alfred Ellenwood Giles, LL.B.	Boston	Resigned 6 February, 1865.

5 November, 1856.

George Noyes	Boston	31 December, 1880.

3 December, 1856.

David Webster Hoyt, A.M.	Brighton	Resgd. 22 November, 1862.
Nathan Henry Chamberlain (Rev.), A.B.	Cambridge	Elected Corresponding Member, 4 April, 1860.
Frank Winthrop Bigelow, A.M., LL.B.	Weston	31 January, 1865.

7 January, 1857.

NAME.	RESIDENCE.	MEMBERSHIP CEASED.
LUKE BROOKS, Jr.	Boston	Resgd. 30 December, 1870.
HENRY MASON BROOKS	Salem	Resigned 5 January, 1861.

4 February, 1857.

ENOCH CARTER ROLFE, M.D.	Boston	Died 27 March, 1875.
JAMES WHYTE MERRIAM	Boston	Resgd. 14 December, 1861.
GEORGE THOMAS THACHER	Dorchester	31 December, 1882.
JOHN LAWRENCE FOX, U.S.N., A.B., M.D.	Charlestown	Died 17 December, 1864.
JASPER HAZEN YORK, M.D.	Boston	Life Member, 1874. Died 7 April, 1874.

4 March, 1857.

WILLIAM WIRT WHITCOMB	Boston	Resigned 12 April, 1884.
JAMES WARHAM CROOKS, A.M.	Springfield	Died 5 August, 1867.
WILLIAM ADAMS RICHARDSON, A.M., LL.B., LL.D.	Lowell.	
ALFRED ABBOTT PRESCOTT	Reading	31 January, 1865.
JOHN BARSTOW	Providence, R.I.	Life Member, 1860. Died 31 March, 1864.
MATTHEW HARVEY, A.M., LL.D.	Concord, N.H.	Died 7 April, 1866.

1 April, 1857.

ARIAL IVERS CUMMINGS, A.M., M.D., LL.B.	Roxbury	Resigned 3 April, 1860.
CHARLES BUNKER	Roxbury	Resgd. 14 November, 1861.
GEORGE WHITE, A.M., LL.B.	Quincy.	

6 May, 1857.

SAMUEL BURNHAM, A.M.	Rindge, N.H.	Died 22 June, 1873.
JOSEPH RICHARDSON (Rev.), A.M.	Hingham	Elected Honorary Member, 2 January, 1861.
EDWARD SPRAGUE RAND, Jr., A.M., LL.B.	Cambridge	Life Member, 1870. 1 October, 1890.
DEAN WILLIS TAINTER	Boston	5 April, 1870.

3 June, 1857.

EDWARD HOLDEN	Roxbury	Resgd. 20 January, 1877.
GEORGE MINOT, A.B., LL.B.	Reading	Died 15 April, 1858.

1 July, 1857.

HIRAM CARLETON, A.M., D.D.	Barnstable	Resigned 19 April, 1870.
EDWARD GRENVILLE RUSSELL (Rev.), A.M.	Cambridge	Resigned 1 July, 1862. Re-elected, 6 November, 1872.

5 August, 1857.

Name.	Residence.	Membership ceased.
Edwin Ruthven Hodgman (Rev.), A. M.	Lynnfield .	5 April, 1870.
And Emerson	Boston . .	Died 3 May, 1871.

2 September, 1857.

Horace Granville Barrows . .	Boston . . .	Resigned 1 January, 1860.
John Brainard Mansfield. . .	Boston . . .	31 December, 1860.
William Emerson Baker . . .	Boston . . .	Life Member, 1863. Died 5 January, 1888.
James Marshall Wilder . .	Boston . . .	Resigned 1 July, 1863.

7 October, 1857.

Francis Low Harding . .	Boston . . .	31 January, 1865.
Elisha Copeland . . .	Boston . . .	Died 8 November, 1864.
Daniel Bates Curtis. . .	Dorchester.	
Daniel Henshaw, A. M. . .	Boston . . .	Elected Corresponding Member, 3 July, 1861.

4 November, 1857.

Jeremiah Colburn, A. M. . . .	Boston . . .	Life Member, 1865. Died 30 December, 1891.
Daniel Jennings Coburn . . .	Boston . . .	Resigned 27 August, 1860.
Winslow Lewis, A. M., M. D. . .	Boston . . .	Life Member, 1863. Died 3 August, 1875.
Ezra Wilkinson, A. M. . .	Dedham . .	Died 6 February, 1882.

2 December, 1857.

Henry Austin Scudder, A. M. .	Boston . . .	Resgd. 27 February, 1862.
Henry Adolphus Miles, A.M., D.D.	Boston . . .	Elected Corresponding Member, 5 December, 1860.
Rufus Wyman	Roxbury . .	31 December, 1865.
David Thayer, A. M., M. D. . .	Boston.	
Peter Ebenezer Vose	Dennysville, Me.	
Thomas Tobey Richmond (Rev.), A. M.	Boston . . .	Resigned 29 May, 1863.

6 January, 1858.

Josiah Quincy, Jr., A. M. . . .	Boston . . .	31 December, 1880.
William Hussey Page, M. D. . .	Boston . . .	31 December, 1880.
Charles Douglas Cleaveland, M. D.	Boston . . .	Died 20 November, 1875.
Thaddeus Allen, A. M.	Boston . . .	Resigned 18 January, 1871.
Strong Benton Thompson . . .	Boston . . .	Died 14 August, 1880.
Joseph Harrison Ward	Boston . . .	Life Member, 1868. Died 12 January, 1888.

NAME.	RESIDENCE.	MEMBERSHIP CEASED.
DAVID BRYANT	Boston . . .	Died 24 September, 1867.
CALVIN PARKMAN HINDS	Boston . . .	Resgd. 15 January, 1877.
FRANCIS BROWN HAYES, A.M. . .	Boston . . .	Life Member, 1875. Died 20 September, 1884.
RICHARD BRIGGS	Boston . . .	31 December, 1880.
CALVIN GUILD, Jr.	Dedham . .	Resgd. 23 September, 1862.
WILLIAM SHERMAN LELAND, A.M.	Roxbury . .	Died 26 July, 1869.
CHARLES STEARNS	Springfield .	Died 11 April, 1860.

3 February, 1858.

JOSIAH KENDALL WAITE (Rev.), A.B.	Fall River . .	Resgd. 31 December, 1861.
WILLIAM ELLIOT WOODWARD . .	Roxbury . .	3 April, 1877.
WILLIAM THOMAS SMITHETT, A.M., D.D.	Boston . . .	Elected Corresponding Member, 7 December, 1859.
FRANCIS SAMUEL DRAKE	Dorchester .	Elected Corresponding Member, 3 February, 1864.
JAMES RIPLEY OSGOOD, A.M. . .	Boston . . .	Resgd. 28 December, 1891.
JOHN SAMUEL HILL FOGG, A.M., M.D.	Boston.	
LANGFORD WHIPPLE LORING . .	Boston . .	6 April, 1869.
EDMUND TUCKER EASTMAN, A.M., M.D.	Boston.	
ALEXANDER HAMILTON RICE, A.M., LL.D.	Boston . . .	Life Member, 1871.

3 March, 1858.

WILLIAM PERKINS APTHORP (Rev.), A.M.	Boston . . .	Resgd. 22 September, 1865.
JOSEPH ADDISON COPP, D.D. . .	Chelsea . .	Died 7 November, 1869.
JAMES BROWNING MILES, A.B., D.D.,	Charlestown .	Resigned 14 October, 1874.
GEORGE EDDY HENSHAW . . .	Cambridge .	Died 20 May, 1862.
JOSIAH WOODBURY HUBBARD . .	Boston . . .	1 October, 1890.
AMOS BAKER	Boston . . .	Resigned 6 January, 1866.
CHARLES BOWKER SHERMAN . .	Boston . . .	5 September, 1865.
THOMAS JOSEPH HAZEN	Dorchester .	Resgd. 16 November, 1861.

7 April, 1858.

JONATHAN PEIRCE	Boston . . .	Died 6 August, 1867.
JOHN DUDLEY PHILBRICK, A.M., D.C.L., LL.D.	Boston . .	Died 2 February, 1886.
JOSIAH ATHERTON STEARNS, A.M., Ph.D.	Boston . . .	Died 8 September, 1883.
HENRY FLAVEL JOHNSON, M.D. .	Southborough	Resgd. 1 November, 1862.

NAME.	RESIDENCE.	MEMBERSHIP CEASED.
LUCIUS ALDEN TOLMAN	Boston . . .	Resgd. 3 December, 1867
EDWARD BUCKNAM MOORE, M. D.,	Boston . .	Died 16 September, 1874.
WILLIAM GRAY WISE.	Lowell . . .	2 March, 1869. Re-elected 7 December, 1881.
JOHN GARDNER WHITE, A. M. . .	Boston . . .	Life Member, 1866.

4 May, 1858.[1]

SAMUEL DANA BELL, A. B., LL. D.	Manchester. N. H.	See Corresponding Roll, 5 May, 1847. Died 31 July. 1868.

5 May, 1858.

NATHAN ALLEN, A. M., M. D., LL. D.	Lowell . . .	Resgd. 1 April, 1861. Re-elected 6 January, 1886.
JOSEPH WHITE, A. B., LL. D. . .	Lowell . . .	Life Member, 1870. Died 21 November, 1890.
DAVID ATHERTON BOYNTON . .	Lowell . . .	31 January, 1865.
JOHN FREDERICK DUNNING . . .	Lowell . . .	Died 27 June, 1862.
FREDERICK WILLIAM CHAPMAN (Rev.). A. M.	Ellington, Conn.	Died 21 July, 1876.
JOHN STEELE TYLER, A. M. .	Boston . . .	Life Member. 1871. Died 20 January, 1876.
WILLIAM ALVORD BURKE, A. M. .	Lowell . . .	Life Member, 1870. Died 28 May, 1887.

2 June, 1858.

FRANKLIN HARVEY SPRAGUE . .	Boston . . .	31 December, 1865.
WILLIAM BATES, A. M.	Boston . . .	31 January, 1865.
THOMAS GAFFIELD	Boston . . .	Resigned 4 January, 1888.
ARON ESTEY FISHER, A. M. . .	Roxbury . .	5 April. 1870.
SAMUEL ABBOTT GREEN, A. M., M. D.	Boston . . .	Life Member, 1870.
NATHAN MUNROE (Rev.), A. M. .	Haverhill . .	Died 8 July, 1866.

7 July, 1858.

EDGAR KIMBALL WHITAKER .	Needham . .	2 March, 1869.
JOHN WILSON CANDLER	Boston . . .	Life Member, 1863.
JOHN SAMUEL MARCH	Boston . . .	3 April, 1877.
HENRY JAMES PRENTISS	Boston . . .	Died 22 April, 1869.
WILLARD MASON HARDING (Rev.), A. M.	Quincy . . .	Resgd. 15 November, 1861.
HUBBARD WIER SWETT	Boston . . .	Resgd. 15 November, 1871.

4 August, 1858.

EDWARD CHIPMAN GUILD (Rev.), A. M.	Boston . . .	5 April. 1870.
HUBBARD WINSLOW DYER BRYANT[2]	Boston . .	Resigned 1 March, 1876.

[1] At a Monthly Meeting of the Board of Directors held 4 May, 1858 : " Judge Samuel Dana Bell of Manchester, N. H., was made a Resident Member." *Directors' Records*, I. 44.

[2] Mr. Bryant, in writing his name, now (1891) omits " Dyer."

6 October, 1858.

NAME.	RESIDENCE.	MEMBERSHIP CEASED.
ALEXANDER WILLIAMS	Boston.	
RICHARD PIKE (Rev.), A.M.. . .	Dorchester .	Died 18 February, 1863.
JOHN KIMBALL ROGERS	Boston . . .	Resgd. 23 November, 1861. Re-elected 3 January, 1883.
JOSEPH BALLARD	Boston . . .	Died 23 November, 1877.
THOMAS BURDETT HARRIS . . .	Charlestown .	Resgd. 28 December, 1861.

3 November, 1858.

STEPHEN EMMONS	Boston . . .	Resgd. 16 January, 1866.
HENRY WYLES CUSHMAN	Bernardston .	See Corresponding Roll, 5 May, 1847. Died 21 November, 1863.
NICHOLAS ALESSANDRE APOLLONIO	Boston . . .	Resigned January, 1870.
JOSEPH BARKER STEARNS . . .	Boston . . .	Resgd. 2 February, 1867.

1 December, 1858.

EDWIN MARTIN STONE (Rev.). . .	Providence, R.I.	Resigned 9 March, 1860.
JOHN RICHARDS, A.B., D.D. . .	Hanover, N.H.	Died 29 March, 1859.
GEORGE CHANDLER, A.B., M.D. .	Worcester . .	Life Member, 1866.
CURTIS CUTLER (Rev.), A.B. . .	Cambridge .	Died 13 October, 1874.

5 January, 1859.

WILLIAM VINCENT HUTCHINGS . .	Gloucester .	Died 26 July, 1888.
FREDERICK WEST HOLLAND (Rev.), A.M.	Dorchester .	Resigned 7 January, 1883.
WILLIAM ESTABROOK FRENCH . .	Boston . . .	5 April, 1870.

2 February, 1859.

ROBERT GOULD, Jr.	Hull	2 March, 1869.
WILLIAM SUMNER APPLETON, A.M., LL.B.	Boston . . .	Life Member, 1864.
JOSHUA PERKINS CONVERSE . . .	Woburn . .	Died 16 March, 1876.
DENZELL MANSFIELD CRANE (Rev.), A.M.	Boston . . .	Resigned 16 October, 1863.

2 March, 1859.

THOMAS OSBORNE RICE (Rev.), A.M.	Brighton . .	Elected Corresponding Member 4 April, 1860.
JOHN SEABURY ELDRIDGE, A.M., LL.B.	Canton . . .	Resigned 3 January, 1871.
THEODORE AUGUSTUS NEAL . . .	Salem . . .	Life Member, 1870. Died 26 October, 1881.
WILLIAM HILTON	Boston . . .	Life Member, 1870. Died 25 December, 1887.

6 April, 1859.

Name.	Residence.	Membership ceased.
WILLIAM PEIRCE	Cambridge	Died 22 May, 1883.

4 May, 1859.

FREDERIC THOMAS BUSH	Boston	Resigned 31 March, 1869.

1 June, 1859.

WASHINGTON GILBERT (Rev.), A.M.	Newton	31 December, 1875.
JOSEPH HOCKEY	Boston	Died 13 October, 1863.

6 July, 1859.

JAMES THURSTON (Rev.), A.M.	Lunenburg	Died 13 January, 1872.
CHARLES HYDE OLMSTED, A.M.	East Hartford, Conn.	Resgd. 11 January, 1871.
BENJAMIN PRATT HOLLIS	Boston	Resgd. 15 November, 1861.
LORENZO SABINE, A.M.	Roxbury	Died 14 April, 1877.

3 August, 1859.

CHARLES FREDERIC GERRY, A.M.	Chelsea	31 December, 1880.
CHARLES CARROLL VINAL (Rev.), A.B.	North Andover	Resigned 29 May, 1861.
AUGUSTUS GILL	Canton	Resigned 14 March, 1864.
EDWARD FRANKLIN EVERETT, A.M.	Charlestown	Life Member, 1862.
HENRY WILSON, A.M., LL.D.	Natick	Died 22 November, 1875.

7 September, 1859.

RALPH SANGER, A.M., D.D.	Dover	Died 6 May, 1860.
WARREN HANDEL CUDWORTH (Rev.), A.M.	Boston	5 April, 1870.
PETER HOBART, Jr.	Boston	Life Member, 1866. Died 15 July, 1879.

21 September, 1859.

WILLIAM FREDERICK GOODWIN, U.S.A., A.M., LL.B.	Concord, N.H.	Died 12 March, 1872.
CHARLES FREDERICK WINSLOW, M.D.	Newton	5 April, 1870.
JOHN KIMBALL WIGGIN	Boston	Died 20 August, 1875.
WILLIAM WARLAND CLAPP, Jr., A.M.	Boston	Life Member, 1870. Died 8 December, 1891.
AUSTIN JACOBS COOLIDGE, A.M., LL.B.	Cambridge.	

5 October, 1859.

JOSEPH HUNT ALLEN	Boston	3 April, 1877.
THOMAS FOSTER WELLS	Roxbury	Resigned 6 May, 1862.

Name.	Residence.	Membership ceased.
George Arthur Simmons . . .	Roxbury . .	Died 26 February, 1884.
William Foster	Boston . . .	Died 25 February, 1863.
George Oliver Sears	Boston.	
Samuel Hobart Winkley (Rev.), A.M.	Boston . . .	Resigned 6 May, 1862.
Alfred Porter Putnam, A.B., D.D.	Roxbury	See 7 March, 1888. Elected Corresponding Member, 7 December, 1864.
John Joseph May	Boston . . .	Life Member, 1870.
Simeon Pratt Adams	Boston . . .	Life Member, 1871. Died 14 August, 1880.

2 November, 1859.

George Gardner Withington (Rev.)	Easton . . .	Resgd. 1 January, 1869.
Adams Ayer (Rev.), A.B. . . .	Charlestown, N. H.	Resgd. 5 October, 1876.
James Freeman Clarke, A.B., D.D.	Jamaica Plain	Life Member, 1869. Died 8 June, 1888.
Edmund Burke Willson (Rev.), A.M.	Salem.	
John Tisdale Bradlee	Boston . . .	Resgd. 17 February, 1875.
James William Thompson, A.B., D.D.	Jamaica Plain	Resigned 16 March, 1861.
George Hughes Hepworth (Rev.)	Boston . . .	Resigned 28 June, 1871.
William Henry Ladd	Lynn . . .	Resgd. 11 December, 1862.
Henry Purkitt Kidder	Boston . . .	Life Member, 1870. Died 28 January, 1886.
John Turner Sargent (Rev.), A.M.	Boston . . .	Resgd. 26 October, 1871. Re-elected 5 February, 1873.
Edward Hamilton	Boston . . .	31 December, 1869.
William Augustus Brewer . .	Cambridge .	Resgd. 30 January, 1874.

7 December, 1859.

John Savillian Ladd, A.M. . .	Cambridge .	Died 5 September, 1886.
Theophilus Parsons, A.M., LL.D.	Cambridge .	Resgd. 26 December, 1872.
Thomas Cushing, A.M.	Boston . . .	Resgd. 27 December, 1875.
Benjamin Chickering	Pittsfield . .	31 December, 1871.
John Sargent	Cambridge .	Died 5 December, 1880.
Joseph Angier (Rev.), A.B. . .	Milton . . .	Resgd. 28 February, 1865.
John Codman Ropes, A.B., LL.B.	Boston.	
Gideon French Thayer, A.M. .	Boston . . .	Died 27 March, 1864.
Gardiner Paine Gates	Medford . .	Resgd. 29 October, 1873.

NAME.	RESIDENCE.	MEMBERSHIP CEASED.
OLIVER BRASTOW DORRANCE . .	Portland, Me.	Died 23 October, 1873.
NATHANIEL BRIGGS BORDEN . .	Fall River .	Died 10 April, 1865.

4 January, 1860.

JAMES GREGORY	Marblehead .	Died 7 October, 1874.
JEFFREY RICHARDSON, Jr. . . .	Boston . . .	Died 6 October, 1860.
JOHN HOPKINS MORISON, A.M., D.D.	Milton.	
THOMAS SIMES DENNETT	Dorchester	Died 12 September, 1863.
EBEN NORTON HORSFORD, A.M. .	Cambridge.	
SAMUEL BATCHELDER, Jr., A.B., LL.B.	Cambridge	Resgd. 10 January, 1876.
WILLIAM AUGUSTUS SAUNDERS . .	Cambridge .	Resgd. 6 December, 1877.
JOHN HARVARD ELLIS, A.M., LL.B.	Charlestown .	Resgd. 30 March, 1862.

1 February, 1860.

GEORGE WINGATE CHASE . . .	Haverhill . .	Resgd. 6 November, 1865.
EBENEZER WEAVER PEIRCE . .	Freetown.	
FREDERICK ALLEN	Westminster .	5 April, 1870.
SAMUEL BLAKE	Dorchester	Died 2 March, 1867.
CHARLES McKENZIE DINSMORE .	Cambridge .	Resgd. 9 January, 1863.
CHARLES CHAUNCY SEWALL (Rev.), A.M.	Medfield . .	Resgd. 12 September, 1865.

15 February, 1860.

NATHANIEL PHILLIPS LOVERING .	Boston . . .	Died 4 October, 1887.
SAMUEL CROCKER COBB	Roxbury . .	Life Member, 1870. Died 18 February, 1891.
JOHN RUGGLES, A.M.	Brighton.	

7 March, 1860.

SOLON WANTON BUSH (Rev.), A.B.	Medfield.	
CLAUDIUS BUCHANAN PATTEN . .	Needham . .	Resgd. 11 December, 1862.
JOHN BUNKER TAYLOR, M.D. . .	Cambridge .	Resgd. 16 November, 1861.

4 April, 1860.

EDWARD AUGUSTUS NEWTON . .	Pittsfield . .	Died 18 August, 1862.
CHARLES STEPHEN LYNCH . . .	Boston . . .	Died 5 April, 1873.
THEOPHILUS CLINTON FRYE . . .	Andover.	
PYNSON BLAKE	Boston . . .	Died 7 January, 1862.
HEZEKIAH EARL	Boston . . .	Resgd. 17 December, 1866.

2 May, 1860.

JOHN HUBBARD WILKINS, A.M. .	Boston . . .	Died 5 December, 1861.
CHARLES BINGLEY HALL	Boston . . .	Life Member, 1863. Died 8 May, 1883.
MOSES POTTER	Boston . . .	Died 13 February, 1865.

6 June, 1860.

NAME.	RESIDENCE.	MEMBERSHIP CEASED.
JOSIAH PORTER, A.M., LL.B. . .	Cambridge .	2 March, 1869.
WILLIAM ALLEN, A.M.	East Bridgewater	31 December, 1887.

11 July, 1860.

GEORGE WILLIAM WHEELWRIGHT	Belmont . .	Died 16 December, 1879.
HENRY WATERMAN FRENCH . . .	Easton.	

5 September, 1860.

ABNER MORSE (Rev.), A.M. . . .	Boston . . .	See Corresponding Roll. 3 June, 1846. Died 16 May, 1865.
HENRY ORIN HILDRETH	Dedham . .	31 December, 1867.
JAMES MONROE KEITH, A.B. . .	Boston.	

3 October, 1860.

EDWARD RUPERT HUMPHREYS, A.M., LL.D.	Cambridge.	
BENJAMIN HUNTOON (Rev.), A.M.	Marblehead .	Died 19 April, 1864.

5 December, 1860.

WILLIAM MOUNTFORD (Rev.) . .	Boston . . .	Resigned 23 January, 1874.
BENJAMIN LEEDS	Brookline . .	Died 8 April, 1866.

2 January, 1861.

HALES WALLACE SUTER, A.M. .	Boston.	
GEORGE ELLIS ALLEN	Newton . .	Resgd. 14 January, 1878.

16 January, 1861.

JOHN HANNIBAL SHEPPARD, A.M. .	Boston . . .	Life Member, 1866. Died 25 June, 1873.
ALDEN SPEARE	Boston . . .	Resigned 22 March, 1870.

6 February, 1861.

CHARLES EDWARD GRISWOLD . .	Boston . . .	Died 6 May, 1864.
ASA HOWLAND	Conway . .	Life Member, 1870. Died 24 June, 1870.
BRADFORD KINGMAN	Brookline . .	Life Member, 1882.

6 March, 1861.

LOUIS ATHANASE SURETTE . . .	Concord . .	3 April, 1877.
ABRAM EDMANDS CUTTER . . .	Charlestown .	Life Member, 1873.
WELLINGTON LA GARONNE HUNT,	Boston . . .	Life Member, 1863. Died 31 October, 1889.

3 April, 1861.

NAME.	RESIDENCE.	MEMBERSHIP CEASED.
SAMUEL JONES SPALDING, A.B., D.D.	Newburyport .	1 July. 1891.
EDWARD MARION ENDICOTT	. . Boston . . .	Resigned 20 March. 1869.

1 May, 1861.

CHARLES WHITLOCK MOORE	. . Boston . . .	Died 12 December, 1873.
SILAS NELSON MARTIN	. . . . Wilmington,N.C.	Life Member, 1871. Died 22 January, 1877.

3 July, 1861.

NEHEMIAH WASHBURN .	. . . . Brookline . .	Life Member, 1863. Died 27 January, 1873.

4 September, 1861.

HUGH MONTGOMERY	. . . . Boston . . .	Life Member, 1863. Died 13 March, 1883.
ABRAHAM ANNIS DAME	. . . . Boston . . .	Died 14 November, 1878.

6 November, 1861.

ELIPHALET JONES	. . . . . Boston . . .	Life Member, 1871. Died 17 March, 1873.

4 December, 1861.

EDMUND FARWELL SLAFTER, A.M., D.D.	Boston . . .	Life Member, 1866.
ABBOTT ELIOT KITTREDGE, A.M., D.D.	Charlestown .	31 December, 1864.

1 January, 1862.

ISAAC EMERY .	. . . . Boston . . .	Life Member. 1870. Died 3 July, 1875.
SELWIN ZADOCK BOWMAN, A.B., LL.B.	Charlestown .	Resgd. 14 January, 1873.

5 March, 1862.

EDWARD WARREN CLARK (Rev.), A.M.	Newton . .	2 March, 1869.

2 April, 1862.

HOLMES AMMIDOWN	. . . . . Boston . . .	Life Member, 1870. Died 3 April, 1883.
STILLMAN PRATT (Rev.), A.B. . .	Middleborough	Died 1 September, 1862.

4 June, 1862.

DORUS CLARKE, A.M., D.D.	. . Waltham . .	Life Member, 1870. Died 8 March, 1884.
SAMUEL PAGE FOWLER	. . . . Danvers . .	Died 15 December, 1888.
KILBY PAGE .	. . . . Jamaica Plain	Died 24 April, 1868.
THEOPHILUS ROGERS MARVIN,A.M.	Boston . . .	Died 9 May. 1882.

2 July, 1862.

Name.	Residence.	Membership ceased.
HENRY MARTYN DEXTER, A.M., D.D., LL.D.	Boston . . .	Died 13 November, 1890.
CHARLES AUGUSTUS BILLINGS SHEPARD	Boston . . .	Died 25 January, 1889.
GEORGE MOUNTFORT [1]	Boston . . .	See Corresponding Roll, 7 March, 1855. Died 28 May, 1884.

6 August, 1862.

WILLIAM FREDERIC MATCHETT .	Brighton.	
ABNER CHENEY GOODELL, Jr., A.M.	Salem . . .	Life Member, 1863.
SAMUEL TRASK PARKER	South Reading	Life Member, 1862. Died 2 June, 1879.
JOHN CUMMINGS, Jr.	Woburn . .	Life Member, 1863.

3 September, 1862.

NICHOLAS HOPPIN, A.B., D.D. . .	Cambridge .	Died 8 March, 1886.
ABEL CUSHING, A.B.	Dorchester .	See Honorary Roll, 6 January, 1847. Died 19 May, 1866.

1 October, 1862.

JOSEPH RICHARDSON	Boston . . .	Died 24 February, 1869.
GEORGE WASHINGTON JONSON, A.B.	Buffalo, N. Y.	Died 3 August, 1880.
OGDEN CODMAN	Boston . . .	31 December, 1880.

5 November, 1862.

JAMES PARKER	Springfield .	Died 2 January, 1874.
JACOB TODD	Boston . . .	2 March, 1869.
HORATIO ALGER, Jr. (Rev.), A.B. .	Cambridge .	January, 1865.

3 December, 1862.

EBENEZER BURGESS, A.M., D.D. .	Dedham . .	Died 5 December, 1870.
CHARLES SUMNER FELLOWS . . .	Bangor, Me. .	Elected Corresponding Member, 3 April, 1878.

7 January, 1863.

WILLIAM BENTLEY FOWLE . . .	Medfield . .	Died 6 February, 1865.
HENRY WELD FULLER, A.M. . .	Roxbury . .	Died 14 August, 1889.

[1] See, respecting the transfer of Mr. Mountfort's name to the Resident Roll, foot-note on page 100, *post.*

NAME.	RESIDENCE.	MEMBERSHIP CEASED.
CHARLES CHASE DAME	Boston	Life Member. 1872.
JOSHUA TUCKER, M.D.	Boston	Resigned 22 March, 1870.
JOHN ADAMS VINTON (Rev.), A.M.	Boston	Life Member. 1863. Died 13 November, 1877.
INCREASE NILES TARBOX, A.M., D.D.	Newton	Died 3 May, 1888.

4 February, 1863.

EDWARD SUMNER ATWOOD, A.M., D.D.	Needham	3 April, 1877.
SAMUEL JENNISON, A.B.	Newton	Resgd. 10 January, 1878.
GUSTAVUS ADOLPHUS SOMERBY	Boston	Died 24 July, 1879.
ABNER AUGUSTUS KINGMAN	Boston	31 December, 1871.
NATHANIEL CURTIS, A.M.	Boston	Life Member. 1870. Died 22 November, 1873.
EPHRAIM LOMBARD	Boston	Resigned December, 1879.
NATHAN BEAN PRESCOTT	Jamaica Plain	2 March, 1869.
WILLIAM BOWLES BRADFORD	Boston	Died 16 April, 1865.
ROBERT CODMAN, A.M., LL.B.	Boston	Life Member. 1870.
THOMAS CHADBOURNE, M.D.	Concord, N.H.	Life Member, 1863. Died 29 April, 1864.
MOSES THOMPSON WILLARD, M.D.	Concord, N.H.	Life Member, 1863. Died 30 May, 1883.
GEORGE CARTER RICHARDSON	Cambridge	Life Member. 1863. Died 20 May, 1886.
WILLIAM CHAUNCEY FOWLER (Rev.), A.M., LL.D.	Durham, Conn.	Died 15 January, 1881.

4 March, 1863.

WILLIAM APPLETON	Boston	Life Member, 1863. Died 10 February, 1877.

1 April, 1863.

THOMAS TOLMAN. A.M.	Boston	Died 20 June, 1869.
CHARLES AUGUSTUS SKINNER (Rev.)	Cambridge	Resigned 12 October, 1874.
JEROME GEORGE KIDDER	Boston	Died 4 November, 1882.
JOHN ALBION ANDREW, A.B., LL.D.	Boston	Life Member, 1863. Died 30 October, 1867.
GINERY TWICHELL	Brookline	Life Member. 1866. Died 23 July, 1883.

6 May, 1863.

PERCIVAL LOWELL EVERETT	Boston	Life Member, 1870.
FRANCIS JOSIAH HUMPHREY, A.M., LL.B.	Boston	Life Member. 1870. Died 9 August. 1883.
GEORGE BATY BLAKE	Boston	Life Member, 1863. Died 6 August, 1875.

NAME.	RESIDENCE.	MEMBERSHIP CEASED.
CHARLES OCTAVIUS WHITMORE . .	Boston . . .	Life Member, 1867. Died 15 November, 1885.
CHARLES CHAUNCY BURR . . .	Newton . .	Life Member, 1863.
CARMI EMERY KING	Boston . . .	Life Member, 1870. Died 16 February, 1890.

3 June, 1863.

EDWARD BUSH	Boston . . .	Died 21 June, 1866.

1 July, 1863.

HENRY LEE, Jr., A. M..	Boston . .	Life Member, 1870.
WILLIAM PHILLIPS TILDEN (Rev.), A. M.	Boston . .	Died 3 October, 1890.
JOHN HOOPER	Boston . . .	Died 7 February, 1866.
ISAAC OSGOOD	Charlestown .	Died 22 June. 1865.
SAMUEL HURD WALLEY, A. M. . .	Boston . . .	Life Member, 1870. Died 27 August, 1877.
JAMES MADISON BEEBE	Boston . . .	Life Member, 1866. Died 9 November, 1875.
WILLIAM VEAZIE	Somerville .	Resigned 31 March, 1869.
JAMES READ	Boston . . .	Life Member, 1863. Died 24 December, 1870.
JOHN NEWTON TURNER	Brookline . .	Died 16 May, 1864.
MARTIN MAY KELLOGG	Boston . . .	Life Member, 1863. Died 7 November, 1889.

5 August, 1863.

MOSES FIELD FOWLER	Boston . . .	Died 15 November, 1888.
NATHANIEL GATES CHAPIN . . .	Brookline . .	Life Member, 1870.
HENRY WARREN	Boston . . .	Resigned 4 January, 1871.

2 September, 1863.

JONATHAN TENNEY, A. M., Ph. D. .	Boscawen, N. H.	Elected Corresponding Member, 6 January, 1869.
HARRISON ELLERY	Boston.	
HENRY GRAFTON CLARK, M. D. .	Boston . . .	Resgd. 12 October, 1876.
JOHN SEAVER HOWARD	Chelsea . .	Died 16 March, 1865.

7 October, 1863.

JAMES BAILEY RICHARDSON, A. B.	Boston . . .	Resgd. 11 January, 1876.
FRANK FIELD FOWLER	Boston . . .	Resigned 19 May, 1868.
ELBRIDGE TORREY	Boston . . .	Resigned 1877.

4 November, 1863.

NAME.	RESIDENCE.	MEMBERSHIP CEASED.
EDWARD STRONG MOSELEY. A. M.	Newburyport	Resigned 9 January, 1866. Re-elected 5 April, 1871.
THOMAS WILLIAM PARSONS, A.M.	Boston . . .	Resigned 14 April, 1873.

2 December, 1863.

AUGUSTUS THORNDIKE PERKINS, A.M., LL. D.	Boston . . .	Life Member, 1870. Died 21 April, 1891.
JOHN TRULL HEARD	Boston . . .	Life Member. 1872. Died 1 December, 1880.
DELORAINE PENDRE COREY . . .	Malden	Life Member, 1871.

3 February, 1864.

WILLIAM WHITWELL	Boston . . .	Died 2 November, 1870.
JOSHUA STETSON	Brookline . .	Died 25 July. 1869.
EDWARD SPRAGUE RAND, A.M., LL. B.	Boston . . .	Life Member. 1865. Died 18 January, 1884.
EBENEZER BREWER FOSTER . . .	Boston . . .	Resigned 12 July, 1875.
HENRY BENJAMIN HUMPHREY . .	Thomaston, Me.	Life Member, 1864. Died 29 February, 1872.
LUCIUS ROOT EASTMAN (Rev.). A.M.	Boston . . .	3 April, 1877.
GEORGE HENRY BROWN	Groton . . .	Died 3 May, 1865.
SOLOMON PIPER	Boston . . .	Died 15 October, 1866.
FRANCIS FRENCH	N. Bridgewater	3 April, 1877.

2 March, 1864.

WILLIAM WADE COWLES	Boston . . .	Resigned 1 January, 1879. See 7 November, 1850.
HALSEY JOSEPH BOARDMAN, A.B. .	Boston . . .	1 October, 1890.
THOMAS WILLIAM SILLOWAY (Rev.), A. M.	Boston.	

6 April, 1864.

FRANKLIN COOLEY WARREN, M.D.	Boston.	
ISRAEL PERKINS WARREN. A.B., D.D.	Boston . . .	Resigned 7 April, 1873.
FREDERIC WILLIAM SAWYER . .	Boston . . .	Died 6 September, 1875.
GEORGE BROOKS BIGELOW, A.B. .	Boston . . .	31 December, 1880.

4 May, 1864.

WILLIAM OGILVIE COMSTOCK . .	Boston . . .	Died 13 April. 1883.
BENJAMIN BARSTOW TORREY . .	Boston . . .	Life Member, 1864.
HARVEY JEWELL, A.B., LL.D. . .	Boston . . .	Died 8 December, 1881.
JOSHUA PUTNAM PRESTON . . .	Boston . . .	Died 10 December, 1876.
EDWARD MONTAGUE CARY . . .	Boston . . .	Died 2 September. 1888.

1 June, 1864.

Name.	Residence.	Membership ceased.
John William Bacon, A.M.	Natick	Died 21 March, 1888.
Charles Eliphalet Lord, A.B., D.D.	Easton	Resgd. 7 December, 1869.
Benjamin Franklin De Costa, D.D.	Charlestown	Elected Corresponding Member, 7 February, 1872.

6 July, 1864.

Henry Colman Kimball, A.B.	Needham	Life Member, 1881.

3 August, 1864.

Usher Parsons, A.M., M.D.	Providence, R.I.	See Corresponding Roll, 1 April, 1845. Died 19 December, 1868.

7 September, 1864.

Andrew Henshaw Ward	Newton	Life Member, 1864.
Charles Colburn	Boston	2 March, 1869.

5 October, 1864.

Francis Leathe, A.B.	New York. N.Y.	2 March, 1869.
Sumner Ellis (Rev.)	Boston	Resgd. 24 February, 1869.

2 November, 1864.

Israel Washburn, Jr., LL.D.	Portland, Me.	Died 12 May, 1883.

7 December, 1864.

Andrew Croswell (Rev.)	Cambridge	Resigned 7 July. 1874.
Charles Endicott	Milwaukee, Wis.	Resgd. 29 December, 1877.

4 January, 1865.

Sylvester Phelps	Milton	Resgd. 4 January, 1871.
Richard Manning Hodges (Rev.), A.M.	Cambridge	Life Member, 1865. Died 10 August. 1878.
Otis Brigham Bullard	Holliston	Life Member, 1877.
Cornelius Newton Bliss	Boston	Life Member, 1870.
Frederick Deane Allen	Boston.	
George Shepard Page	Brooklyn, N.Y.	Resgd. 19 December, 1876.
Elbridge Wason	Boston	Life Member, 1865. Died 20 August, 1887.

1 February, 1865.

Albert Blodgett Weymouth, A.M., M.D.	Boston	Resgd. 15 November, 1873.
Edward Chase Wilson	Brookline	Life Member, 1865.
Stephen Fairbanks	Boston	Died 10 September, 1866.

1 March, 1865.

NAME.	RESIDENCE.	MEMBERSHIP CEASED.
EDWARD JACOB FORSTER, M.D. .	Charlestown .	Resgd. 29 December, 1888.
GEORGE JENCKES FISKE . . .	Boston . . .	Life Member, 1865. Died 4 December, 1868.
EBENEZER PORTER DYER (Rev.). A. B.	Somerville . .	Resgd. 29 January, 1871.
EDWARD HILL JUDKINS [1] . . .	Boston.	
NAHUM JONES	Dorchester.	
CHARLES TILTON DUNCKLEE, A.M., LL.B.	Boston . . .	31 December, 1872.
EDWIN FORSTER ADAMS	Charlestown .	Died 16 August, 1871.
AUSTIN SUMNER	Boston . . .	Died 14 October, 1879.
WILLIAMS LATHAM, A.B.	Bridgewater .	Life Member, 1871. Died 6 November, 1883.
WILLIAM S ANDERSON [2]	Boston . . .	Resigned 2 March, 1869.
WILLIAM HENRY DENNET . . .	Boston . . .	Resgd. 2 December, 1867.
WILLIAM VAUGHAN SPENCER . .	Boston . . .	Resigned 22 March, 1870.
ABRAHAM AVERY, A.M.	Boston . .	Life Member, 1870.

5 April, 1865.

ALFRED MUDGE	Boston . . .	Life Member, 1871. Died 14 August, 1882.
CHARLES WESLEY TUTTLE, A.M., Ph.D.	Boston . . .	Life Member, 1868. Died 17 July, 1881.

3 May, 1865.

EDWARD STANLEY WATERS, A.M.	Salem . . .	31 December, 1884.

7 June, 1865.

AZEL AMES, Jr., M.D.	Chelsea . .	31 December, 1880.
GEORGE WILLIAM BALDWIN, A.B.	Boston.	

5 July, 1865.

SAMUEL WALLEY CREECH, Jr. . .	Boston . .	1 October, 1890.
CHARLES CARLETON COFFIN, A.M.	Boston.	
ELISHA TYSON WILSON	Boston . . .	Life Member, 1871. Died 18 June, 1872.

2 August, 1865.

NATHAN CROSBY, A.M., LL.D. .	Lowell . . .	Died 11 February, 1885.
ASA MILLETT, M.D.	Bridgewater.	
ADEL BALL, M.D.	Boston . . .	Died 3 November, 1876

[1] Mr. Hill's name was changed (in 1872) to Edward Judkins Hill.

[2] Mr. Anderson had no middle name, but used "S" as a designation.

6 September, 1865.

NAME.	RESIDENCE.	MEMBERSHIP CEASED.
FRANCIS PARKMAN, A.B., LL.B., LL.D.	Boston . . .	Life Member, 1871.
ALBERT CLARKE PATTERSON (Rev.), A.M.	Jamaica Plain	Life Member, 1871. Died 21 October, 1874.
ALEXANDER HAMILTON BULLOCK, A.B., LL.D.	Worcester . .	Life Member. 1868. Died 17 January, 1882.

4 October, 1865.

EDWIN HOLBROOK SAMPSON . .	Boston . . .	Life Member, 1870.
JOSEPH LYMAN HENSHAW . . .	Boston . . .	Died 8 July, 1873.

1 November, 1865.

EDWIN THOMPSON	Charlestown .	Life Member, 1871. Died 17 June. 1886.
ADIN BALLOU UNDERWOOD, A.B.	Newton . .	Life Member, 1872. Died 14 January, 1888.
SAMUEL LOTHROP THORNDIKE. A.M., LL.B.	Boston.	

6 December, 1865.

HAMPDEN CUTTS, A.M. . . .	Brattleboro', Vt.	Died 28 April, 1875.
SAMUEL DORR. A.B.	Boston . . .	3 April, 1877.
THOMAS RICKER LAMBERT, A.M., D.D.	Charlestown .	Life Member, 1866. Died 4 February, 1892.
CALVIN LINCOLN (Rev.), A.M. .	Hingham .	Resigned January, 1867.

3 January, 1866.

ALEXANDER JOHNSTON STONE, M.D.. LL.D.	Newton . .	Life Member, 1870.
JOHNSON GARDNER, M.D. .	Providence, R.I.	Died 12 December, 1869.

7 February, 1866.

THOMAS TEMPLE ROCKWARD . .	Holliston . .	Died 11 October, 1872.
ABEL BLANCHARD BERRY . . .	Randolph . .	3 April, 1877.
GEORGE RUSSELL	Boston . . .	Resgd. 27 December, 1882.
HENRY EDWARDS	Boston . . .	Died 24 September, 1885.
JOHN CLARK MERRIAM . . .	Boston . . .	Resigned 4 January, 1871.
ALBERT WILLIAM LOVERING .	Roxbury . .	Resigned 4 January, 1870.

7 March, 1866.

HENRY LINSLEY HOBART . . .	Boston . . .	Died 23 July, 1873.
ROBERT HOOPER, Jr.	Boston . . .	Died 21 September, 1883.
DAVID QUIMBY CUSHMAN (Rev.), A.B.	Hubbardston .	Life Member, 1871. Died 13 October, 1889.
WILLIAM WHITMAN	Cambridge.	

Name.	Residence.	Membership ceased.
John Parker Towne, A. B.	Edgerton Rock, Wis.	Life Member, 1868.
Henry Bott Groves	Salem	Died 16 April, 1877.
David Clapp	Boston.	

4 April, 1866.

Henry Fitch Jenks (Rev.), A. M.	Boston	Life Member, 1880.
Henry Jones (Rev.), A. M.	Bridgeport, Conn.	Life Member, 1870. Died 9 November. 1878.
Appleton Howe, A. M., M. D.	Weymouth	Died 10 October, 1870.
John Emory Hoar, A. M.	Brookline.	
Henry White Pickering, A. M.	Roxbury	Resigned 7 May, 1892.

2 May, 1866.

Henry Lyon, A. M., M. D.	Charlestown	Life Member. 1870.
Benjamin Winslow Harris, LL. B.	East Bridgewater.	
Abraham Firth	Brookline	Resgd. 18 February, 1875.
George Silsbee Hale, A. M.	Boston.	
John Alden Loring, A. B.	Boston	Resigned 11 April, 1872.

6 June. 1866.

Edward Emerson Bourne, A. M., LL. D.	Kennebunk, Me.	Died 23 September, 1873.
Albert Louis Richardson	Woburn	31 December. 1884.
George Henry Preble, U. S. N.	Charlestown	Life Member. 1869. Died 1 March. 1885.

1 August, 1866.

Albert Harrison Hoyt. A. M.	Boston	Life Member. 1868.
William James Foley	Boston.	
Joshua Eddy Crane	Bridgewater	31 December, 1872.
Dexter Harrington Chamberlain	West Roxbury	Life Member. 1870. Died 17 September, 1887.

5 September, 1866.

Elisha Clark Leonard	New Bedford.	

3 October. 1866.

Charles Augustus Ranlett, Jr.	New York, N.Y.	Died 6 February, 1874.
Ephraim Williams Allen (Rev.), A. B.	Haverhill	Resgd. 11 January, 1882. Re-elected 3 October, 1883.
Austin Spencer Pease	Boston	Resgd. 5 November, 1874.

5 December. 1866

Francis Bush, Jr.	Boston	Died 16 August, 1874.

5

2 January, 1867.

Name.	Residence.	Membership ceased.
George Washington Simmons	Boston	Resigned 23 March, 1870.
Samuel Curtis Clarke	Newport, R. I.	
Nehemiah Brown	Boston	3 April, 1877.
James Monroe Battles	Dedham	Life Member, 1877.

6 February, 1867.

John Tyler Hassam, A.M.	Boston	Life Member, 1880.
George Henry Everett	Boston	Resgd. 23 December, 1872.
Albert Hale Plumb, D.D.	Chelsea	Resgd. 22 October, 1873.
James Phillips Bush	Boston	Resigned 22 March, 1870.
Charles Henry Woodwell	Boston	Died 31 January, 1871.
William Henry Brooks, A.M., D.D.	Chelsea	Resgd. 10 January, 1870.
Cyrus Woodman, A.M.	Cambridge	See Corresponding Roll, 5 September, 1855. Life Member, 1869. Died 30 March, 1889.
Christopher Cushing, A.M., D.D.	North Brookfield	Died 23 October, 1881.
Eliakim Littell	Brookline	Died 17 May, 1870.

6 March, 1867.

Levi Reed	Abington	Died 18 October, 1869.
Lewis Brooks Bailey	Boston	Died 18 November, 1888.
Charles Woolley	Waltham	Died 30 October, 1886.
William Emery Bicknell	Boston	Resigned 4 June, 1880.
Randolph Marshall Clark, A.M.,	Boston	Died 11 September, 1873.
Joseph Maria Finotti (Rev.)	Brookline	Died 10 January, 1879.
James Hill Fitts (Rev.)	West Boylston.	
William Stowe	Boston.	

3 April, 1867.

Erastus Worthington, A.B., LL.B.	Dedham	31 December, 1884.
Lemuel Pope	Cambridge.	Life Member, 1874.

5 June, 1867.

Jeremiah Otis Wetherbee	Boston	1 July, 1891.

3 July, 1867.

William Henry Osborne	East Bridgewater.	3 April, 1877.
Charles Augustus Jones	Roxbury	Resigned 1876. Re-elected 2 March, 1881.
John Fairfield Rich	Boston	Died 3 November, 1872.

NAME.	RESIDENCE.	MEMBERSHIP CEASED.
ROBERT BOODY CAVERLY, LL.B.	Lowell . . .	31 December, 1885.
ABRAHAM BAILEY SHEDD . . .	Brookline .	3 April, 1877.

7 August, 1867.

DARIUS DANIELS FARNUM . . .	Woonsocket.R.I.	Life Member, 1876.
WILLIAM SEWELL GARDNER, A.M.	Lowell . . .	Life Member, 1884. Died 4 April, 1888.
BENJAMIN FRANKLIN HAM . . .	Winchester .	Resgd. 19 October, 1874.

4 September, 1867.

THOMAS HARRISON DUNHAM, Jr. .	Boston . . .	Resigned 11 July, 1874.
OLIVER HAZARD PERRY	Newport, R.I.	Resgd. 10 November, 1873.
CHARLES LEVI WOODBURY . . .	Boston.	

2 October. 1867.

NATHANIEL TOPLIFF ALLEN . . .	Newton . .	Resgd. 15 January, 1877.
HAYDEN BROWN	West Newbury	Life Member, 1870.
THOMAS McCULLOCK HAYES, A.B.	Boston . . .	Died 1 February, 1869.

6 November. 1867.

OLIVER CHACE	Fall River .	Resgd. 20 February, 1873.
ANDREW WIGGIN	Dedham . .	Resgd. 23 December, 1876.
EBENEZER TORREY. A.M. . . .	Fitchburg .	Life Member, 1870. Died 3 September, 1888.
JOHN CLARK. A.M.	Boston . . .	Died 22 July, 1870.

4 December, 1867.

WILLIAM ROGERS	Boston . . .	Died 15 January, 1869.
NATHANIEL GALE	Chelsea . .	3 April, 1877.
JOHN JACOB LOUD, A.M.	Weymouth .	Life Member, 1874.
JOHN WATSON TAYLOR	Boston . . .	31 December, 1880.

1 January. 1868.

EDWARD SWAIN DAVIS . . .	Lynn . . .	Died 7 August. 1887.
JOTHAM SEWALL CHASE	Boston . . .	Resgd. 25 November, 1872.
JOHN BIGELOW	Boston . . .	Died 2 January, 1878.
EDWARD TOBEY BARKER	Charlestown.	
HENRY HERBERT EDES	Charlestown .	Life Member, 1871.
ROBERT HOOPER. A.M.	Boston . . .	Died 5 March, 1868.
WILLIAM SMITH PEABODY . . .	Boston . . .	Life Member, 1870. Died 10 July. 1877.
ALONZO ADAMS HAMILTON . . .	Boston . . .	31 December, 1880.

5 February, 1868.

NAME.	RESIDENCE.	MEMBERSHIP CEASED.
THOMAS SHERWIN, A.M.	Dedham	Died 23 July, 1869.
MATTHIAS DENMAN ROSS	Boston	Life Member, 1870.
JACOB SLEEPER	Boston	Life Member, 1871. Died 31 March, 1889.
AARON DAVIS WELD	West Roxbury	Life Member, 1870. Died 24 April, 1889.
MOSES PARSONS STICKNEY (Rev.), A.M.	Boston	Resgd. 24 January, 1878.
CHARLES LOUIS FLINT. A.M., LL.B.	Boston	Life Member, 1870. Died 26 February, 1889.
JOHN DAVIS SWEET (Rev.)	Billerica	Died 7 August, 1869.
WILLIAM WOODBRIDGE WILSON	Brookline	Resigned January, 1870.
ISAAC DAVENPORT HAYWARD	Boston	31 December, 1871.
CHARLES EMELIUS LAURIAT	Boston	Resgd. 28 February, 1874.
JONATHAN FRENCH, A.M.	Boston	Life Member, 1868.

4 March, 1868.

JAMES FROTHINGHAM HUNNEWELL, A.M.	Charlestown	Life Member, 1870.
JOTHAM GOULD CHASE	Boston	Life Member, 1870. Died 5 December, 1884.
JAMES FOUQUET WILLIAMS	Brookline	Died 25 October, 1886.
GEORGE WATSON PRESCOTT	Charlestown	Resigned 5 January, 1875.
ANSON PARKER HOOKER, A.B., M.D.	Cambridge	Died 31 December, 1873.

1 April, 1868.

JOHN MARSHALL BROWN, A.M.	Portland, Me.	
JOHN COFFIN JONES BROWN	Boston	Life Member, 1876.
WILLIAM THOMAS HOLLIS	Plymouth	Resigned 22 March. 1870.
NEWELL ALDRICH THOMPSON	Boston	Life Member, 1870. Died 10 April, 1874.
HENRY VEASEY WARD	Boston	Died 14 March, 1873.
THOMAS PRENTISS ALLEN (Rev.), A.B.	Newton	Died 26 November, 1868.
ARTHUR FRENCH TOWNE, LL.B.	Brookline	Life Member, 1870.
JOHN DENNISON BALDWIN, A.M.	Worcester	Died 8 July, 1883.

6 May, 1868.

ROBERT MORRIS BAILEY	Boston	Died 5 March, 1892.
THOMAS RICHARDSON	Boston	Died 16 December, 1872.
THEODORE POOLE HALE	Boston	Died 1 March, 1879.

NAME.	RESIDENCE.	MEMBERSHIP CEASED
SAMUEL HIDDEN WENTWORTH, A.M., LL. B.	Boston . . .	Life Member, 1868.
WILLIAM OTIS JOHNSON, A.B., M.D.	Boston . .	Died 17 August, 1873.
EDWARD YOUNG WHITE	Cambridge .	Resgd. 23 January, 1877.
EDWARD SILAS TOBEY, A.M. . .	Boston . . .	Life Member, 1870. Died 29 March, 1891.
JOHN GARDNER	Boston .	Resigned January, 1877.
WILLARD FRANCIS MALLALIEU, A.M., D.D.	Boston .	Life Member, 1873.
OTIS NORCROSS	Boston . .	Life Member, 1868. Died 5 September, 1882.
HILAND HALL, LL.D. . .	Bennington, Vt.	Life Member, 1871. Died 18 December, 1885.
BENJAMIN HINMAN STEELE, A.B. .	St. Johnsbury, Vt.	Resigned 1 January, 1873.
HENRY BOYNTON, A.M., M.D. . .	Woodstock, Vt.	Resigned January, 1871.
GILBERT ASA DAVIS	Felchville, Vt.	31 December, 1871.
HIRAM ORCUTT, A.M., LL.D. . .	Lebanon, N.H.	Resigned 2 July, 1874.
LUKE POTTER POLAND, LL.D. . .	St. Johnsbury, Vt.	31 December, 1880.
PETER THACHER WASHBURN, A.M.	Woodstock, Vt.	Died 7 February, 1870.
CHARLES HORACE HUBBARD . .	Springfield, Vt.	Resgd. 24 October, 1874.
THOMAS WENTWORTH HIGGINSON, A.M.	Newport, R.I.	

3 June, 1868.

WILLIAM HATHAWAY CLARKE LAWRENCE	Boston . . .	Resgd. 17 October, 1881.
EDWARD BROOKS, A.M.	Boston . . .	Life Member, 1871. Died 11 April, 1878.
ARIEL STANDISH THURSTON . . .	Elmira, N.Y.	
ASAHEL PECK, LL.D.	Montpelier, Vt.	Life Member, 1871. Died 18 May, 1879.
DAVID PARSONS HOLTON, A.M., M.D.	New York, N.Y.	Life Member, 1868. Died 8 June, 1883.
CHARLES HENRY BELL, A.M., LL.D.	Exeter, N.H.	Life Member, 1870.
JOHN JAMES BELL, A.M., LL.B. .	Exeter, N.H.	
JOHN MAJOR SHIRLEY, A.M. . .	Andover, N.H.	Resigned 23 May, 1876.

1 July, 1868.

ELIJAH SMALLEY	Boston . . .	31 December, 1885.
SILVANUS JENKINS MACY	New York, N.Y.	Life Member, 1870.
MOSES GRANT DANIELL, A.M. . .	Roxbury.	
ELMER TOWNSEND	Boston . . .	Died 13 April, 1871.
JOHN GREENLEAF WHITTIER, A.M., LL.D.	Amesbury .	Life Member, 1868.

2 September, 1868.

NAME.	RESIDENCE.	MEMBERSHIP CEASED.
CHARLES MARTIN, U.S.N., M.D. .	Cambridge .	Resigned 22 January, 1881.
JOHN LEE WATSON, U.S.N., A.M., D.D.	Boston . . .	Resigned 27 October, 1871. Elected Corresponding Member, 6 March, 1872.
JOHN DEARBORN TOWLE	Boston . . .	3 April, 1877.
EDWARD PAYSON BURNHAM . . .	Saco, Me. . .	Life Member, 1868.

7 October, 1868.

JOHN HARVEY WRIGHT, U.S.N., A.B., M.D.	Boston . . .	Died 26 December, 1879.
GEORGE WHITEFIELD AVERY, M.D.	New Orleans, La.	Life Member, 1878.

4 November, 1868.

GEORGE WILLIAM BOND, A.M.. .	West Roxbury	Resigned 3 April, 1878.
ALVAH CROCKER	Fitchburg . .	Life Member, 1868. Died 26 December, 1874.
CHARLES FREDERICK BRADFORD, A.M.	Randolph . .	Resigned 1 January, 1873.

2 December, 1868.

CHARLES HENRY STANLEY DAVIS, M.D.	Meriden, Conn.	31 December, 1883.
WILLIAM ALFRED BUCKINGHAM, LL.D.	Norwich, Conn.	Life Member, 1868. Died 5 February, 1875.
GEORGE LINCOLN	Hingham . .	31 December, 1880.
PLINY HOLTON WHITE (Rev.), A.M.	Coventry, Vt. .	Life Member, 1868. Died 24 April, 1869.

6 January, 1869.

DAVID GREENE HASKINS, A.M., D.D.	Cambridge.	
DAVID GREENE HASKINS, Jr., A.M., LL.B.	Cambridge.	
JOHN FOSTER	Boston . . .	Life Member, 1869.
NATHAN HAGAR DANIELS . . .	Boston . . .	3 April, 1877. Re-elected 5 March, 1890.
JOHN RUSSELL BARTLETT, A.M. .	Providence, R.I.	Died 28 May, 1886.
EDWARD IRVING DALE	Boston . . .	Resigned 24 March, 1881.
ELEAZER BURBANK LORING . . .	Boston . . .	31 December, 1882.
ALBERT BOYD OTIS, A.M., LL.B.. .	Boston.	
JAMES MORTON BALLARD, A.B. .	Boston . . .	Resigned 2 June, 1876.
STEPHEN NICKERSON STOCKWELL, A.M.	Boston . . .	Resigned January, 1873.
IRA PERLEY, A.M., LL.D. . . .	Concord, N.H.	Died 26 February, 1874.
AMBROSE EASTMAN, A.M. . . .	Boston . . .	Resgd. 18 February, 1881.
ELIPHALET WICKES BLATCHFORD	Chicago, Ill. .	Life Member, 1869.

3 February. 1869.

NAME.	RESIDENCE.	MEMBERSHIP CEASED.
FRANCIS MINOT WELD, A.B. . .	West Roxbury	Life Member, 1870. Died 4 February, 1886.
EUGENE ANTHONY VETROMILE, D.D.	Bangor, Me. .	Life Member, 1871. Died 23 August, 1881.
JAMES PILLSBURY LANE (Rev.), A.B.	Andover . .	Resigned 23 June, 1877.
FRANK WAYLAND REYNOLDS . .	West Roxbury	Resigned 25 March, 1881.
ELISHA POMEROY CUTLER, Jr. .	Charlestown .	Resigned 8 July, 1890.
GEORGE CRAFT	Brookline . .	Life Member, 1871. Died 21 July, 1883.
CARLOS SLAFTER (Rev.), A.M. .	Dedham . .	Life Member, 1869.
PETER BUTLER	Boston . . .	Life Member, 1869.
ROLAND GREENE USHER . .	Lynn . . .	Life Member, 1875.
ARTHUR LIVERMORE, A.M. . . .	Lowell . . .	31 December, 1872.
HIRAM BURR CRANDALL . . .	Boston . . .	Resigned 13 July, 1875.
CHARLES COWLEY, LL.D. . . .	Lowell . . .	Life Member, 1870.
SIDNEY CAPEN BANCROFT . . .	Peabody . .	3 April, 1877.

3 March, 1869.

GEORGE EDWIN EMERY	Lynn . . .	31 December, 1884.
AUGUSTUS PARKER	Roxbury.	
WILLIAM PICKERING HAINES, A.B., LL.D.	Boston . . .	Died 2 July, 1879.
JAMES ADAMS, Jr.	Charlestown .	Life Member. 1870.
BENJAMIN EDWARD BATES, A.B. .	Boston . . .	Life Member, 1873. Died 14 January, 1878.
BENJAMIN FRANKLIN BURGESS .	Boston . . .	Life Member, 1869.
GEORGE HORATIO KUHN . . .	Boston . . .	Life Member. 1869. Died 21 February, 1879.
NATHANIEL THAYER, A.M. . . .	Boston . . .	Life Member, 1869. Died 7 March, 1883.
WILLIAM THOMAS	Boston . . .	See 7 April. 1847. Life Member, 1869. Died 19 June, 1872.
CHARLES WILLIAM RAISBECK . .	Boston . . .	Died 15 September, 1872.
EDWARD LAWRENCE	Charlestown .	Life Member, 1869. Died 17 October, 1885.
JAMES LOVELL LITTLE .	Boston . . .	Life Member, 1869. Died 19 June. 1889.
EBEN DYER JORDAN	Boston . . .	Life Member. 1869.
ALBERT FEARING	Boston . . .	See 5 May, 1847. Life Member. 1869. Died 24 May, 1875.

NAME.	RESIDENCE.	MEMBERSHIP CEASED.
BENJAMIN BAKER DAVIS. . . .	Brookline . .	Died 23 August, 1877.
WILLIAM WARREN TUCKER, A.M.	Boston . . .	Life Member, 1869. Died 26 November, 1885.

7 April, 1869.

AARON CHARLES BALDWIN, A.B..	Boston . . .	Resigned 3 May, 1873.
GEORGE DANIELS	Milford, N. H.	Life Member, 1871. Died 5 February, 1881.
WILLIAM HYDE	Ware . . .	24 June, 1888.
HENRY MARTYN CLARKE . .	Boston . . .	Life Member, 1870.
WALTER COOPER GREEN . .	Boston . . .	Died 25 April, 1875.
DANIEL DENNY	Boston . . .	Died 9 February, 1872.
HENRY AUGUSTUS RICE . .	Dorchester .	Life Member, 1870.
FRANCIS BASSETT, A.M. . . .	Boston . . .	Life Member, 1869. Died 25 May, 1875.
WILLIAM POPE	Brookline . .	Resigned 10 May, 1873.
CHARLES AUGUSTUS STEARNS .	Boston . . .	Life Member, 1882.
SAMUEL HENRY GOOKIN . .	Boston . . .	Life Member, 1870.
NATHAN DURFEE, A.M., M.D. . .	Fall River .	Life Member, 1871. Died 6 April, 1876.
JAMES ALEXANDER DUPEE . .	Boston . . .	Died 18 October, 1886.
HENRY PHILEMON HAVEN . .	New London, Conn.	Life Member, 1870. Died 30 April, 1876.
SAMUEL RUSSELL PAYSON .	Boston . . .	Life Member, 1871.
CHARLES WILLIAM FREELAND . .	Boston . . .	Life Member, 1870. Died 25 December, 1883.

5 May, 1869.

JOSHUA WINSLOW PEIRCE . . .	Portsmouth, N. H.	Died 10 April, 1874.
ISAAC BORDEN CHACE.	Fall River .	Died 17 October, 1887.
JAMES WARREN SEVER, A.M. . .	Boston . . .	Life Member, 1869. Died 16 January, 1871.
GEORGE BERNARD DRAKE . . .	Boston . . .	Resigned 3 January, 1871.
GEORGE BIGELOW CHASE, A.M.	Boston . . .	Life Member, 1870.
CHARLES DUDLEY HOMANS, A.M., M.D.	Boston . . .	Life Member, 1869. Died 1 September, 1886.
JOHN LOCKE ALEXANDER, A.M.. M.D.	Belmont . .	Life Member, 1870. Died 9 November, 1890.
WARREN EVERETT EATON . . .	Charlestown .	1 July, 1891.

2 June, 1869.

CHARLES HENRY GUILD	Somerville .	Life Member, 1870.
BENJAMIN APTHORP GOULD FULLER, A.M.	Boston . . .	Died 24 January, 1885.

1 September, 1869.

Name.	Residence.	Membership ceased.
Nathan Burnett Chamberlain .	Newton . .	Resigned 7 July. 1874.
Samuel Foster Upham	Boston . . .	Resgd. 16 January, 1877.
Otis Milton Humphrey, M.D. .	Boston . . .	Resgd. 12 November, 1874.
Joseph Gay Eaton Larned, A.M.	New York. N.Y.	Died 3 June, 1870.
John Allen Lewis	Boston . . .	Died 2 November, 1885.
Josiah Burnham Kinsman, LL.B.	Boston . . .	Resgd. 19 January, 1877.
George Stevens, A.M.	Lowell . . .	Life Member, 1870. Died 6 June, 1884.
Asa Dodge Smith, A.M., D.D., LL.D.	Hanover, N.H.	Life Member, 1870. Died 16 August, 1877.

6 October, 1869.

Francis Jewett Parker	Boston.	

3 November, 1869.

Arthur Mason Knapp, A.M. . .	Boston . . .	Resigned 14 July, 1875.
Peter Harvey, A.M.	Boston . . .	Died 27 June. 1877.
Samuel Cutler (Rev.)	Hanover . .	Life Member. 1870. Died 17 July, 1880.
Roger Averill	Danbury, Conn.	Life Member, 1871. Died 9 December. 1883.
Richard Anson Wheeler . . .	Stonington. Conn.	
Amasa Walker, LL.D.	North Brookfield	See 5 February. 1851. Life Member. 1871. Died 29 October, 1875.
Marshall Jewell, A.M. . . .	Hartford, Conn.	Died 10 February, 1883.
John Benjamin Lewis, M.D. . .	Hartford, Conn.	31 December, 1873.
Richard Pratt Spencer . .	Saybrook, Conn.	
Elbridge Henry Goss	Melrose.	
Oliver Henry Perry, A.M. . .	Southport,Conn.	Died 27 March. 1882.
Alexander Hamilton Holley .	Salisbury, Conn.	Life Member, 1869. Died 2 October, 1887.
Simeon Eben Baldwin, A.M., LL.D.	New Haven, Conn.	Life Member, 1872.
Benjamin Douglas . .	Middletown, Conn.	
Jeremiah Lemuel Newton, A.M.	Boston . . .	Resigned 12 January, 1877.
Edwin Holmes Bugbee	Killingly. Conn.	Life Member, 1870.

1 December. 1869.

Calvin Brown	Mare Island Navy Yard.Cal.	31 December. 1884.
David Temple Packard (Rev.), A.M.	Brighton . .	Life Member. 1871. Died 28 November, 1880.

NAME.	RESIDENCE.	MEMBERSHIP CEASED.
WILLIAM MASON CORNELL, A.M., M.D., D.D., LL.D.	Boston . . .	See 6 February, 1856. See Corresponding Roll, 2 November, 1859. Life Member, 1876.
SAMUEL RUGGLES SLACK (Rev.) .	Boston . . .	See Corresponding Roll, 1 July, 1857. Resgd. 8 December, 1880.
JOHN GREENLEAF ADAMS (Rev.) .	Lowell . .	Resigned January, 1874.

5 January, 1870.

NAME.	RESIDENCE.	MEMBERSHIP CEASED.
JOHN DANIEL RUNKLE, A.M., S.B., PH.D., LL.D.	Boston . . .	Life Member, 1870.
EZRA FARNSWORTH	Boston . . .	Life Member, 1870. Died 4 July, 1890.
TIMOTHY WADSWORTH STANLEY .	New Britain, Conn.	Life Member, 1872.
FRANCIS ADINO PAGE, U.S.A. . .	Washington, D.C.	31 December, 1872.
NATHAN COOLEY KEEP, M.D., D.M.D.	Boston . . .	Died 11 March, 1875.
GEORGE LYMAN BARR	Medford . .	Died 1 April, 1877.
DUDLEY RICHARDS CHILD . . .	Boston . . .	Life Member, 1879. Died 12 May, 1883.
LEARNED HEBARD	Lebanon, Conn.	Died 30 October, 1877.
CHARLES WILLIAM ROMNEY . .	Boston . . .	Life Member, 1877.
GEORGE PARTRIDGE SANGER, A.M., LL.B.	Cambridge .	Life Member, 1872. Died 3 July, 1890.
HENRY SMITH	Boston . . .	Life Member, 1870. Died 7 May, 1881.
MARTIN PARRY KENNARD . . .	Brookline.	
ALVIN LANE FISHER	Charlestown .	3 April, 1877.
JAMES FRANCIS CLARK HYDE . .	Newton . .	Resgd. 19 February, 1877.
DELANO ALEXANDER GODDARD, A.M.	Boston . . .	Died 11 January, 1882.
BENJAMIN PIERCE CHENEY, A.M. .	Boston . . .	Life Member, 1870.

2 February, 1870.

NAME.	RESIDENCE.	MEMBERSHIP CEASED.
SAMUEL BAKER RINDGE	Cambridge .	Life Member, 1883. Died 3 May, 1883.
LEBBEUS STETSON	Somerville .	Died 13 October, 1890.
SAMUEL ADAMS	Milton . . .	Life Member, 1871. Died 3 January, 1879.
HENRY LILLIE PIERCE, A.M. . .	Dorchester .	Life Member, 1870.
WILLIAM WILLDER WHEILDON .	Charlestown .	Died 7 January, 1892.

Name.	Residence.	Membership Ceased.
Arthur John Clark Sowdon, A.M., LL.B.	Boston.	
Albert Decatur Spaulter Bell	Boston . .	Life Member, 1872.
Robert Bennett Forbes . . .	Boston . . .	Died 23 November, 1889.
Clement Hugh Hill, A.M. . .	Boston . . .	31 December, 1886.
William Edward Perkins, A.B., LL.B.	Boston . . .	3 April, 1877.
Joshua Wyman Wellman, A.M., D.D.	Newton	Life Member, 1871.
Edmund Hatch Bennett, A.M., LL.D.	Taunton . .	31 December, 1883. Re-elected 1 October, 1890.

2 March, 1870.

Lilley Eaton	Wakefield . .	See Corresponding Roll, 4 August, 1847. Died 16 January, 1872.
Ezekiel Russell, A.M., D.D.. .	Randolph.	
Oliver Mayhew Whipple . . .	Lowell . . .	See Corresponding Roll, 5 May, 1852. Died 26 April, 1872.
William Pelby Cabot	Boston . . .	Resigned January, 1886.

6 April, 1870.

Daniel Franklin Child .	Boston . . .	Life Member, 1870. Died 18 October, 1876.
William Temple	Woburn . .	Died 18 March, 1886.
William Lawton	New Rochelle, N. Y.	Life Member, 1875. Died 27 April, 1881.
Daniel Denison Slade, A.B., M.D.	Newton.	
Elbridge Gerry Kelley, M.D. .	Newburyport .	Resgd. 31 December, 1875.
Francis Jaques	Boston . . .	Life Member, 1870. Died 17 December, 1884.
David Dunlap Stackpole . . .	Boston . . .	Life Member, 1870. Died 11 March, 1879.
William Barrett	Nashua, N. H.	Resigned 20 July, 1874.
Winfield Scott Smith . . .	Washington, D. C.	31 December, 1880.
Charles Greenwood Pope, A.B.	Somerville .	3 April, 1877.
John Wilkes Hammond, A.B., LL.D.	Cambridge .	6 November, 1889.
Alexis Caswell, A.M., D.D., LL.D.	Providence R.I.	Died 8 January, 1877.
William Holcomb Webster, A.M., LL.B.	New Britain, Conn.	Life Member, 1874.

NAME.	RESIDENCE.	MEMBERSHIP CEASED.
WILLIAM GAMMELL, A.M., LL.D.	Providence. R.I.	See Corresponding Roll, 1 September, 1847. Life Member. 1872. Died 3 April, 1889.
WILLIAM GREENE, A.M.	Warwick, R.I.	Life Member, 1871. Died 24 March, 1883.
EBENEZER BANCROFT TOWNE . .	Raynham . .	Died 30 June, 1885.
OTIS CLAPP	Boston . . .	Died 18 September, 1886.
WILLIAM RICHARD CUTTER . . .	Woburn.	
SILAS AXTELL CRANE, A.M., D.D.	East Greenwich, R.I.	Died 16 July, 1872.
AUSTIN WILLIAMS BENTON . . .	Brookline . .	Life Member, 1871.
WILLIAM TURELL ANDREWS, A.M.	Boston . . .	See 5 August, 1846. Life Member, 1870. Died 24 November, 1879.
ALVIN ADAMS	Watertown .	Life Member, 1870. Died 1 September, 1877.

4 May. 1870.

NAME.	RESIDENCE.	MEMBERSHIP CEASED.
GEORGE WASHINGTON WARE, Jr., A.M., LL.B.	Belmont . .	Died 12 February, 1890.
THOMAS DAVIS TOWNSEND . .	Boston . . .	Life Member. 1870. Died 18 January, 1880.
DANIEL KIMBALL	Boston . . .	Life Member. 1870. Died 21 June. 1874.
WILLIAM EDWARD COFFIN . . .	Boston . . .	Life Member, 1870.
HORATIO HOLLIS HUNNEWELL . .	Needham . .	See 4 August, 1847. Life Member. 1871.
ALMERIN HENRY WINSLOW . . .	Chicago, Ill. .	Died 10 May, 1886.
JAMES HENRY BEAL	Boston . . .	Life Member, 1871.
JOHN WOOD BROOKS	Milton . . .	Life Member, 1870. Died 16 September, 1881.
LYMAN NICHOLS	Boston . . .	Life Member, 1871. Died 26 August. 1878.
NATHAN MATTHEWS	Boston . . .	Life Member, 1870.
ROWLAND HAZARD, A.M. . . .	Providence. R I.	
CALEB FISKE HARRIS, A.M. . .	Providence, R.I.	Life Member, 1872. Died 2 October. 1881.
SIDNEY SMITH RIDER	Providence, R.I.	Resgd. 22 December. 1882.
WILLIAM CLAFLIN, LL.D. . . .	Newton . .	Life Member, 1873.
WILLIAM PERKINS	Boston . . .	Life Member, 1871. Died 13 July, 1887.
JOHN HEARD	Boston . . .	Life Member, 1870.
OAKES AMES	Easton . . .	Life Member, 1871. Died 8 May, 1873.

NAME.	RESIDENCE.	MEMBERSHIP CLASED.
THOMAS WILLIAMS BICKNELL, A. M.	Barrington, R. I.	Resigned 2 April, 1888.
JOHN STRATTON WRIGHT	Boston . . .	Life Member, 1871. Died 29 June, 1874.
EBEN WRIGHT	Boston . . .	Life Member, 1871. Died 1 April, 1881.
BENJAMIN FRANKLIN NOURSE . .	Boston . . .	Life Member, 1870.
GEORGE PARKMAN DENNY . . .	Boston . . .	Life Member, 1870. Died 23 January, 1885.
LEONARD THOMPSON . . .	Woburn . .	Life Member, 1872. Died 28 December, 1880.
HAMILTON ANDREWS HILL, A. M. .	Boston . . .	Fees commuted, 1891.
LUTHER LOUD HOLDEN	Boston . .	31 December, 1874.

1 June, 1870.

NAME.	RESIDENCE.	MEMBERSHIP CLASED.
GEORGE WILLIAMS PRATT. A. M. .	Boston . . .	Died 14 January, 1876.
NATHAN BOURNE GIBBS	Boston . . .	Life Member, 1870. Died 5 December, 1880.
SOLOMON ROBINSON SPAULDING	Boston . . .	Life Member, 1870. Died 31 August, 1874.
THOMAS CRANE WALES	Easton . . .	Life Member, 1871. Died 11 December, 1880.
WILLIAM BROWN SPOONER . .	Boston . . .	Life Member, 1870. Died 28 October, 1880.
NATHANIEL JOHNSON RUST . .	Boston . . .	Life Member, 1872.
WILLIAM ENDICOTT, Jr., A. M. . .	Boston . . .	Life Member, 1870.
SAMUEL JOHNSON	Boston . . .	Life Member, 1870.
LEWIS RICE	Boston . . .	Life Member, 1870. Died 16 March, 1877.
OLIVER AMES	Easton . . .	Life Member, 1873. Died 9 March, 1877.
AARON HEYWOOD BEAN	Boston . . .	Life Member, 1870.
EDMUND PITT TILESTON	Boston . . .	Life Member, 1870. Died 7 June, 1873.
JOSIAH MOORE JONES	Boston . . .	Life Member, 1871. Died 23 April, 1884.
ALBERT THOMPSON	Boston . . .	Life Member, 1871. Died 9 September, 1882.
FRANCIS MARSHALL JOHNSON . .	Boston . . .	Life Member, 1871. Died 6 July, 1878.
OLIVER DITSON	Boston . . .	Life Member, 1870. Died 21 December, 1888.
FRANKLIN KING	Boston . . .	Life Member, 1871.
EBENEZER DALE	Boston . . .	Life Member, 1871. Died 3 December, 1871.

NAME.	RESIDENCE.	MEMBERSHIP CEASED.
FRANCIS DANE	Chelsea . .	Life Member, 1873. Died 30 July, 1875.
GEORGE HASWELL PETERS . . .	Boston . . .	Life Member, 1870. Died 20 December, 1889.
WILLIAM COWPER PETERS, A. M. .	West Roxbury	Life Member, 1870.
NATHAN ROBBINS	Boston . . .	Life Member, 1871. Died 5 September, 1888.
STEPHEN PRESTON RUGGLES . .	Boston . . .	Life Member, 1871. Died 28 May, 1880.
BENJAMIN SEWALL	Boston . . .	Life Member, 1870. Died 12 October, 1879.
ABRAHAM THOMPSON LOWE, M. D.	Boston . . .	Life Member, 1871. Died 4 July, 1888.
BENJAMIN FRANKLIN STEVENS . .	Boston . . .	Life Member, 1870.
FREDERICK JONES	Boston . . .	Life Member, 1871. Died 7 June, 1887.
JOHN SMITH FOGG	Boston . . .	Life Member, 1871. Died 16 May, 1892.
WILLIAM STEVENS HOUGHTON . .	Boston . . .	Life Member, 1870.
SAMUEL ATHERTON	Boston . . .	Life Member, 1871.
ALFRED HUBBARD BATCHELLER .	Boston . . .	Life Member, 1870. Died 22 December, 1891.
DAVID SNOW	Boston . . .	Life Member, 1870. Died 12 January, 1876.
CALEB STETSON	Boston . . .	Life Member, 1871. Died 25 January, 1885.
JOHN PARMELEE ROBINSON . . .	Boston . . .	Life Member, 1870. Died 5 August, 1882.
EBENEZER TRESCOTT FARRINGTON	Boston . . .	Life Member, 1870. Died 6 August, 1880.
ARIEL LOW	Boston . . .	Life Member, 1870. Died 5 January, 1886.
JOHN WOOLDREDGE	Lynn . . .	Life Member, 1870. Died 7 October, 1891
MINOT TIRRELL	Weymouth .	Life Member, 1871. Died 26 December, 1881.
THOMAS LAMB	Boston . . .	Life Member, 1870. Died 25 October, 1887.
NATHANIEL CUSHING NASH . . .	Boston . .	Life Member, 1878. Died 31 August, 1880.
JOHN EMERY LYON, A. M. . . .	Boston . . .	Life Member, 1871. Died 11 April, 1878.
JOSEPH SAMUEL ROPES, A. M. . .	Boston . . .	Life Member, 1870.
ANDREW TOWNSEND HALL . . .	Boston . . .	Life Member, 1871. Died 22 November, 1875.
PHILIP HENRY WENTWORTH . .	Danvers . .	Life Member, 1870. Died 10 April, 1886.

Name.	Residence.	Membership ceased.
Charles Merriam	Boston	Life Member, 1871.
Warren Fisher, Jr.	Boston	Life Member, 1871.
William Fletcher Weld	Boston	Life Member, 1870. Died 30 November, 1881.
Thomas Dennie Quincy	Boston	Life Member, 1870. Died 18 March, 1881.
Avery Plumer	Boston	Life Member, 1871. Died 27 April, 1887.
John Hill	Boston	Life Member, 1870.
Gardner Chilson	Mansfield	Life Member, 1870. Died 21 November, 1877.
Gerry Whiting Cochrane	Boston	Life Member, 1870. Died 1 January, 1884.
George Warren Harding	Boston	Life Member, 1870. Died 22 July, 1887.
James Wheaton Converse	Newton	Life Member, 1871.
Elisha Slade Converse	Malden	Life Member, 1870.
Daniel Baxter Stedman	Boston	Life Member, 1871.
Thomas Edward Chickering	Boston	Life Member, 1870. Died 14 February, 1871.
Leonard Bond Harrington	Boston	Life Member, 1871.
William Taylor Glidden	Boston	Life Member, 1871.
James Cogswell Converse	Abington	Life Member, 1871.
Benjamin Shreve	Salem	Life Member, 1871.
John Gallison Tappan	Boston	Life Member, 1871. Died 29 August, 1883.
John Newton Denison	Boston	Life Member, 1870.
James Wallace Black	Boston	Resigned March, 1880.
James Haughton	Boston	Life Member, 1870. Died 2 January, 1888.
Josiah Giles Bachelder	Brookline	Life Member, 1870. Died 10 August, 1882.
Royal Elisha Robbins	Boston	Life Member, 1871.
Aaron Claflin Mayhew	Milford	Life Member, 1873. Died 26 September, 1880.

7 September, 1870.

Supply Clap Thwing	Boston	Life Member, 1871. Died 4 June, 1877.
Jonathan Preston	Boston	Life Member, 1871. Died 3 July, 1888.
Thomas Dennie Quincy, Jr.	Boston	Life Member, 1870.
Benjamin Greene Smith	Cambridge	Life Member, 1872.
Henry Oxnard Preble	Charlestown	Died 24 May, 1871.
John Adams Buttrick	Lowell	Died 31 March, 1879.
Edwin Wright, A. M.	Boston.	

5 October, 1870.

NAME.	RESIDENCE.	MEMBERSHIP CEASED.
EDWARD GRIFFIN PORTER (Rev.), A.M.	Lexington.	
GEORGE WASHINGTON WARREN, A.M.	Charlestown .	Life Member, 1872. Died 13 May, 1883.
HORACE PARNELL TUTTLE, A.M. .	Georgetown, D.C.	Resigned 13 July, 1874.
NATHANIEL PAINE	Worcester.	

2 November, 1870.

CHARLES EDWIN ALLEN	Cambridge .	3 April, 1877.
JOHN ALFRED POOR, A.M. . . .	Portland, Me.	Died 5 September, 1871.
ALEXANDER MCKENZIE, A.M., D.D.	Cambridge .	Resigned 25 June, 1874. Re-elected 1 Oct., 1890.
CHARLES EDWARD GRINNELL (Rev.), A.M., LL.B.	Charlestown .	Resigned 1 May, 1877.
JOHN NOYES MORSE	Lexington . .	Resgd. 29 December, 1874.

7 December, 1870.

GEORGE BROWN KNAPP, A.M. . .	Newton.	
DANIEL EDWIN DAMON	Plymouth . .	31 December, 1880.
WILLIAM CARVER BATES	Boston . . .	31 December, 1885.
JOHN SHERBURNE SLEEPER . . .	Boston . . .	Died 14 November, 1878.
JAMES HUMPHREYS UPHAM . . .	Boston . . .	Resgd. 31 December, 1880.

4 January, 1871.

ALEXANDER STRONG	Boston . . .	Life Member, 1871. Died 26 June, 1881.
GEORGE NEWTON THOMSON, M.D.	Boston . . .	Life Member, 1874.
EDWARDS AMASA PARK, A.B., D.D., LL.D.	Andover.	
CYRUS HENRY TAGGARD	Boston . . .	Life Member, 1872.
WILLIAM RICHARDS LAWRENCE, M.D.	Boston . . .	Life Member, 1872. Died 20 September, 1885.
JONATHAN TOWNE	Milford, N.H.	Died 10 February, 1874.
HENRY AUGUSTUS GOWING . . .	Boston.	

1 February, 1871.

FRANK FORBES BATTLES	Lowell . . .	Died 19 September, 1889.
ALBERT FORSTER DAMON . . .	Philadelphia, Pa.	Died 23 March, 1887.
ETHAN NELSON COBURN	Charlestown .	Life Member, 1871.
ENOCH REDINGTON MUDGE . . .	Boston . . .	Life Member, 1871. Died October, 1881.
DAVID HENRY BROWN, A.B. . .	Boston . . .	Life Member, 1880.

NAME.	RESIDENCE.	MEMBERSHIP CEASED.
MARCUS DAVIS GILMAN	Newton . .	Resgd. 26 January, 1886.
CHARLES BRADLEY	Providence, R.I.	Resgd. 17 November, 1873.
WILLIAM GIBBONS PRESTON . .	Boston . . .	Life Member, 1871.
CHARLES EDWARD NOYES . . .	Jamaica Plain	Resigned 7 January, 1887.

1 March, 1871.

GEORGE HENRY MARTIN	Bridgewater .	Resigned 1 January, 1887.
ELISHA BASSETT	Boston . . .	Life Member, 1871.
ALEXANDER HAMILTON VINTON, A.M., M.D., D.D.	Boston . . .	See Corresponding Roll. 6 July, 1859. Died 26 April, 1881.
NATHANIEL WING TURNER . . .	Boston . . .	Life Member, 1871.
JAMES REYNOLDS KNOTT . . .	Boston . . .	Life Member, 1871.
CHARLES AMASA HEWINS . . .	West Roxbury.	
ALFRED FAWCETT	Chelsea . .	Life Member, 1871.
EZRA HAWKES	Chelsea . .	Life Member, 1871.

5 April, 1871.

LEVI PARSONS MORTON, LL.D. .	New York, N.Y.	Life Member, 1871.
MOSES CONANT WARREN . . .	Brookline . .	Life Member, 1872. Died 1 October, 1890.
DANIEL WALDO SALISBURY . . .	Boston . . .	Died 18 August, 1890.
WILLIAM GASTON, A.M., LL.D. .	Boston.	
WILLIAM SMITH CLARK, A.M., Ph.D., LL.D.	Amherst .	Died 9 March, 1886.
SAMUEL BATCHELDER	Cambridge .	Died 5 February, 1879.
AMBROSE HASKELL WHITE . . .	Boston . . .	Life Member, 1871. Died 3 June, 1881.
EDWARD RUSSELL	Boston . . .	Life Member, 1871.
ALEXANDER CLAXTON CARY . .	Boston.	
JOSEPH TEEL SWAN	Neponset . .	Resigned 13 July, 1875.
SAMUEL ELWELL SAWYER . . .	Boston . . .	Life Member, 1873. Died 15 December, 1889.
JAMES EDWARD ROOT	Boston . . .	Died 20 September, 1875.
WILLIAM CLEAVES TODD, A.B. .	Boston . . .	Life Member, 1871.
EDWARD STRONG MOSELEY, A.M.	Newburyport .	See 4 November, 1863. Life Member, 1871.
BENJAMIN HEBER RICHARDSON . .	Boston . . .	31 December, 1875.

3 May, 1871.

JONATHAN MASON	Boston . . .	See 6 February, 1845. Died 21 February, 1884.
HENRY ELMER TOWNSEND, A.M., M.D.	Boston . . .	31 December, 1883.
LEONARD AUGUSTUS JONES, A.B., LL.B.	Boston . . .	Resigned 13 January, 1877.

7 June, 1871.

NAME.	RESIDENCE.	MEMBERSHIP CEASED.
CHARLES COTESWORTH PINCKNEY WATERMAN	Sandwich . .	Died 22 November, 1884.
GEORGE PUNCHARD (Rev.), A.M..	Boston . . .	Died 2 April, 1880.
JOHN MINOR BRODHEAD, M.D.. .	Washington, D.C.	Died 22 February, 1880.
WALTER HASTINGS	Charlestown .	Died 28 October, 1879.
FRANKLIN HUNT	Boston.	
HERMAN FOSTER	Manchester .	Life Member, 1871. Died 17 February, 1875.
JOSEPH BEALE GLOVER	Boston.	
WALTER TITUS AVERY A.B. . .	New York, N.Y.	Life Member, 1871.

6 September, 1871.

EDWARD RUSSELL COGSWELL, A.M., M.D.	Cambridge.	
HENRY KNOX THATCHER, U.S.N.. .	Winchester .	Died 5 April 1880.
JOHN CALVIN DODGE, A.M., LL.D.	Boston . . .	Died 17 July, 1890.
EBENEZER CLAPP	Boston . . .	Died 12 June, 1881.
WILLIAM TOLMAN CARLTON . . .	Boston . . .	Died 28 June, 1888.
FREDERICK WARREN GODDARD MAY	Boston.	
FRANCIS EVERETT BLAKE . . .	Boston . . .	Fees commuted, 1888.
GEORGE FABER CLARK (Rev.) . .	Mendon . .	See Corresponding Roll, 7 March, 1855. Life Member, 1872.
EDMUND JAMES BAKER	Boston . . .	Died 15 January, 1890.
CLINTON WARRINGTON STANLEY, A.B.	Manchester, N.H.	Died 1 December, 1884.

4 October, 1871.

JOHN PRENTICE ROGERS	Boston . . .	Resigned 19 March, 1880.

1 November, 1871.

JOHN STAPLES LOCKE	Boston . . .	3 April, 1877.
JOSEPH WARREN TUCKER . . .	Roxbury . .	Died 21 April, 1885.

6 December, 1871.

GEORGE THOMAS LITTLEFIELD . .	Charlestown .	Life Member, 1877.
THOMAS MINNS	Boston . . .	Life Member, 1885.

3 January, 1872.

WILLIAM GOOLD	Windham, Me.	Resgd. 29 December, 1886.
EDWARD WINSLOW HINCKS . . .	Cambridge.	

NAME.	RESIDENCE.	MEMBERSHIP CEASED.
STEPHEN GRANT DEBLOIS . . .	Boston .	Life Member, 1886. Died 5 April, 1888.
QUINCY BICKNELL	Hingham . .	Life Member, 1872.
HORACE DENNISON BRADBURY . .	Cambridge .	Life Member, 1872.
ISAAC LIVERMORE	Cambridge .	Life Member, 1872. Died 9 November, 1879.
HENRY COOK . .	. . Cambridge	Resigned 1 June, 1882.

6 March, 1872.

RANDALL GARDNER BURRELL . .	Boston.	
PETER THACHER, A. M.	Newton.	
ELI WASHBURN	Bridgewater .	Life Member, 1874. Died 21 December, 1879.
HEMAN ROWLEE TIMLOW (Rev.), A.M.	Walpole . .	31 December, 1880.
FRANCIS VOSE PARKER	Boston.	
JOHN FORRESTER ANDREW, A. B., LL. B.	Boston.	
HORATIO NELSON PERKINS, A.B. .	Melrose	Died 3 July, 1883.

3 April, 1872.

WILLIAM CUSHING, A. B.	Newburyport .	Died 15 October, 1875.
LAWRENCE BROWN CUSHING . .	Newburyport.	
DAVID PERKINS PAGE	Newburyport .	Died 6 February, 1874.
GEORGE WINSLOW THACHER . .	Boston . .	Resgd. 15 November, 1874.

1 May, 1872.

WILLIAM MAKEPEACE THAYER (Rev.), A. B.	Franklin.	
HENRY FITZGILBERT WATERS, A.M.	Salem . .	Fees commuted, 1890.

5 June, 1872.

JOSEPH FOWLER JENNISON (Rev.), A. M.	Canton . . .	Resigned April, 1875.
GEORGE MILLARD ELLIOTT . . .	Lowell . . .	31 December, 1884.
WILLIAM KENT	Boston . . .	31 December, 1875.

4 September, 1872.

HUGH DAVIS McLELLAN . . .	Gorham, Me.	Died 9 December, 1878.
BYRON ANASTASIUS BALDWIN . .	St. Louis, Mo.	Life Member, 1872.
GEORGE EDWIN LINCOLN . . .	Newton . .	Died 14 December, 1881.
JOHN BOYNTON WILSON	Charlestown .	31 December, 1880.

2 October, 1872.

NAME.	RESIDENCE.	MEMBERSHIP CEASED.
GEORGE DOWDALL JOHNSON (Rev.), A.B.	Newburyport .	Resigned 5 October, 1875.

6 November, 1872.

GEORGE TOLMAN	Boston . . .	31 December, 1880.
EDWARD GRENVILLE RUSSELL (Rev.), A.M.	Cambridge .	See 1 July, 1857. Died 25 February, 1880.

1 January, 1873.

JOHN CODMAN HURD, A.M. . . .	Boston . . .	Resgd. 11 January, 1881.
CHARLES POMEROY OTIS, A.M., Ph.D.	Boston . . .	Resigned 8 January, 1887.
SAMUEL ADAMS DRAKE	Boston . . .	Resgd. 23 January, 1877.
JOHN NATHANIEL BARBOUR . .	Cambridge .	31 December, 1887.
GEORGE WILLIAM GORDON . . .	Boston . . .	Life Member, 1873. Died 19 November, 1877.

5 February, 1873.

WARREN PRESCOTT ADAMS . . .	Boston . . .	3 April, 1877.
JOSEPH ADAMS SMITH, U.S.N., LL.B.	Boston . . .	Life Member, 1873.
FREDERIC BEECHER PERKINS, A.M.	Boston . .	See Corresponding Roll, 1 April, 1863. Resgd. 17 Septem'r, 1878.
FRANCIS SKINNER, A.B.	Boston . . .	3 April, 1877.
WILLIAM ALBERT PARKER, U.S.N.	Boston . . .	Died 24 October, 1882.
HENRY HARRISON SPRAGUE, A.M.	Boston.	
JOHN TURNER SARGENT (Rev.), A.M.	Boston . . .	See 2 November, 1859. Died 26 March, 1877.

5 March, 1873.

WILLIAM GORDON MEANS . . .	Boston . . .	Life Member, 1882.
BENJAMIN HOLT TICKNOR, A.M. .	Boston.	
ELLERY CHANNING BUTLER (Rev.).	Beverly	Resgd. 11 January, 1877.
JOHN TODD MOULTON	Lynn.	
RICHARD BLISS, Jr.	Cambridge .	31 December, 1880.
ROBERT HENRY EDDY	Boston . . .	Life Member, 1873. Died 13 May, 1887.

2 April, 1873.

FREDERICK COLEMAN SANFORD .	Nantucket . .	Died 13 August, 1890.
JAMES MADISON USHER . . .	Boston . . .	31 December, 1880.
SAMUEL LEONARD CROCKER, A.M.	Taunton . .	Life Member, 1873. Died 10 February, 1883.

7 May, 1873.

NAME.	RESIDENCE	MEMBERSHIP CEASED.
JOHN PHILLIPS PAYSON	Chelsea . .	31 December, 1888.
BENJAMIN BELCHER RUSSELL .	Boston . . .	1 July, 1891.
FRANCIS HENRY LEE	Salem.	
ALEXANDER STARBUCK	Waltham . .	1 October, 1890.
JOSIAH WHITNEY BARSTOW, A. B., M. D.	Flushing, N. Y.	
JOHN BROOKS FENNO	Boston.	

4 June, 1873.

WALTER LLOYD JEFFRIES, A. B., LL. B.	Boston .	Resgd. 27 December, 1882.

3 September, 1873.

SAMUEL PIERCE LONG, A. M. . .	Boston . . .	Died 24 April, 1879.
NATHANIEL FOSTER SAFFORD, A.B.	Milton . . .	Life Member, 1873. Died 22 April, 1891.
GEORGE WILLIAM GREEN (Rev.) .	Boston . . .	31 December, 1880.
WILLIAM BERRY LAPHAM, A. M., M.D.	Augusta, Me.	Resigned 23 June, 1890.
GEORGE COGSWELL. A.M., M.D. .	Bradford . .	Life Member, 1874.

1 October, 1873.

FRANCIS WALKER BACON . . .	Boston . . .	Died 13 January, 1886.
THEODORE PARKER ADAMS, A. B. .	Boston.	
GEORGE TAYLOR PAINE	Providence, R. I.	Life Member, 1875.
ISAAC CHAPMAN BATES, A.M. . .	Paris, France .	Life Member, 1873. Died 24 September, 1875.

5 November, 1873.

SERENO DICKINSON CLARK (Rev.), A. B.	Temple, N. H.	Resgd. 14 December, 1882.
DONALD FRASER GRANT	Boston . . .	3 April, 1877.
JAMES HEMPHILL JONES, U.S.N. .	Charlestown .	Life Member, 1873. Died 17 April, 1880.

7 January, 1874.

JOSEPH BURBEEN WALKER, A.M.	Concord, N. H.	
AMOS STONE	Everett.	
JOSEPH WILLIAMSON, A.M. . . .	Belfast, Me.	
SAMUEL LANE BOARDMAN . . .	Augusta, Me. .	31 December, 1884.
JOHN ROGERS, A.M.	Boston . . .	Died 15 June, 1884.

4 February, 1874.

Name.	Residence.	Membership ceased.
William Rufus Mann	Sharon.	
Otis Drury	Boston . . .	Died 2 October, 1883.
Francis Henry Brown, A.M., M.D.	Boston . . .	Resgd. 17 November, 1875. Re-elected 5 December, 1888.

4 March, 1874.

Robert Gibson Molineaux . .	Boston . . .	Resigned 18 May, 1881.
George Augustus Whiting . .	Charlestown .	31 December, 1887.
William Bliss Hincks, A.M. . .	Bridgeport, Conn.	Resigned 15 March, 1875.
Charles Andrew Reed, A.B. . .	Taunton . .	31 December, 1880.
Alfred Gowing Carter . . .	Woburn . .	31 December, 1882.

1 April, 1874.

Charles Francis Swift	Yarmouth . .	31 December, 1880.
Joseph Whitcom Porter . . .	Burlington, Me.	31 December, 1886.
Daniel Augustus Rogers . . .	Chicago, Ill. .	Life Member, 1875. Died 29 December, 1876.
William Gordon Weld	Boston . . .	Life Member, 1877.
Sereno Dwight Nickerson, A.M., LL.B.	Boston.	
Thomas William Clarke, A.B., LL.B.	Boston . . .	1 July, 1891.

6 May, 1874.

Joseph Jesse Cooke	Providence, R.I.	Life Member, 1877. Died 8 July, 1881.
William Rogers Taylor, U.S.N.	Boston . .	Died 14 April, 1889.
David Miller Balfour	Boston . . .	Resgd. 31 December, 1888
Elias Hasket Derby, A.M. . .	Boston . . .	Died 31 March, 1880.
James Walker Austin, A.M., LL.B.	Boston . . .	Life Member, 1878.
John Milton Hawks, M.D. . .	Hyde Park .	31 December, 1880.
John Oscar Norris, S.B. . . .	Melrose . .	31 December, 1884.

3 June, 1874.

Henry Willard Bragg, A.B. .	Charlestown .	Resigned April, 1880.
Alanson Wilder Beard . . .	Boston.	

2 September, 1874.

Frank Edwin Hotchkiss . . .	New Haven, Conn.	1 October, 1890.

4 November, 1874.

Name.	Residence.	Membership ceased.
Abbott Lawrence, A. M., LL. B.	Boston .	Resgd. 18 December, 1883. Re-elected 1 October, 1890.
John Haven Dexter	Boston . .	Died 31 December, 1876.
Samuel James Bridge, A.M. . .	Boston . . .	See 3 July, 1850.
Samuel Richardson Knox . .	Everett . .	Died 20 November, 1883.

2 December, 1874.

Henry Washington Benham, U. S. A.	Boston	Elected Corresponding Member, 1 June, 1881.
George Monroe Endicott . . .	Canton . . .	Fees commuted, 1891.
Daniel Thomas Vose Huntoon .	Canton . . .	Died 15 December, 1886.

6 January, 1875.

Gustavus Vasa Fox	Boston . .	Life Member, 1875. Died 29 October, 1883.
Ebenezer Coolbroth Milliken, M. D.	Boston . .	Life Member, 1876. Died 3 November, 1889.
Janus Granville Elder . . .	Lewiston, Me.	31 December, 1883.
George Madison Bodge, A.M., D. B.	Westbrook, Me.	
William Low Weston	Danvers	Died 1 February, 1889. See 6 August, 1856.

3 February, 1875.

Albert Lewis Richardson. . .	Boston . . .	Life Member, 1875.

3 March, 1875.

Eben Francis Stone, A.M., LL.B.	Newburyport.	
George Perkins Elliot . . .	Billerica . .	Resigned 7 October, 1880.
Horatio Smith Noyes, A.B. . .	Newton . .	Died 10 August, 1883.
William Crowninshield Waters	Boston . . .	31 December, 1883.
George Lucien Davis	North Andover	Life Member, 1875. Died 23 December, 1891.
David Oakes Clark	Milton . . .	Life Member, 1875. Died 13 December, 1883.

7 April, 1875.

David McCanie Parker, M.D. .	Boston . . .	Resgd. 3 January, 1885.
Howland Holmes, A.M., M.D. .	Lexington.	
Ralph Haskins.	Boston . . .	31 December, 1880.
William Bullard Durant, A. M., LL. B.	Cambridge.	
Charles Lewis Hutchins (Rev.), A.M.	Medford . .	31 December, 1880.

5 May, 1875.

Name.	Residence.	Membership ceased.
John Boyd, A.M.	Winchester, Conn.	Died 1 December, 1881.

2 June, 1875.

Nathaniel Carter Towle, M.D.	Brookline	Resigned 29 May, 1876.
Constantine Canaris Esty, A.M.	Framingham	31 December, 1886.
Benjamin Franklin Tweed, A.M.	Cambridge.	
Sidney Brooks, A.B.	Boston	Died 25 March, 1887.
Phineas Bates, Jr.	Boston	31 December, 1887.
Henry Walker, A.B.	Boston	1 October, 1890.
John Collins Warren, A.B., M.D.	Boston.	
Warren Emerson	Boston	1 July, 1891.
William Thomas Lambert	Charlestown	Life Member, 1875.
Henry Edward Waite	Newton.	
Henry Ware Holland, S.B., LL.B.	Cambridge	Life Member, 1881.
Stephen Shepley	Fitchburg	Died 18 January, 1880.
John Taylor Clark	Boston	Died 30 October, 1880.
Reuben Rawson Dodge	Sutton	31 December, 1880.
Justin Allen, A.B., M.D.	Topsfield	Life Member, 1883.
Edward Avery	Braintree.	
William Henry Wilder	Brookline	Resgd. 8 December, 1891.

1 September, 1875.

Henry Allen Hazen, A.M., D.D.	Billerica.	
Waldo Adams	Boston	Died 9 March, 1892.
John Phelps Putnam, A.M., LL.B.	Boston	Died 4 January, 1882.
Thomas Bellows Peck, A.B.	Walpole, N.H.	Resgd. 22 January, 1890.
Artemas Bowers Muzzey, A.M., D.D.	Cambridge	Died 21 April, 1892.
Cheever Newhall	Boston	Died 8 April, 1878.

6 October, 1875.

John Davis Ames	Fall River	31 December, 1888.
Joseph Russell Bradford, A.M.	Boston	Resgd. 3 January, 1883.
Arthur Martineau Alger, LL.B.	Boston	31 December, 1886.
Grindall Reynolds (Rev.), A.M.	Concord.	

3 November, 1875.

Benjamin Allen Chace	Fall River	31 December, 1880.
Beverley Oliver Kinnear, M.D.	Boston	Resigned January, 1889.
Charles Cotesworth Beaman (Rev.)	Boston	Died 4 July, 1883.

Name.	Residence.	Membership ceased.
CHARLES WESLEY SLACK	Boston . .	Life Member, 1877. Died 11 April, 1885.
SAMUEL EVERETT TINKHAM, S.B. .	Malden . .	Resgd. 30 December, 1881.

1 December, 1875.

HENRY CHARLES THACHER . . .	Yarmouth.	
JOSIAH LITTLE HALE, A.M., M.D. .	Boston.	
ARTHUR WEBSTER TUFTS	Boston . . .	Resgd. 6 February, 1879.
CHARLES WILLARD ALLEN . . .	Chelsea .	Resgd. 20 November, 1884.

5 January, 1876.

CHARLES PINCKNEY HOLBROOK NASON (Rev.). A.M.	Chelsea . .	Resgd. 31 December, 1891.
AUGUSTUS RAMSAY BAYLEY . . .	Cambridge.	
OLIVER BLISS STEBBINS	Boston.	
ARTHUR GREENWOOD FULLER . .	Boston . . .	31 December, 1885.
JOHN HASKELL BUTLER, A.B. . .	Somerville .	Resigned 5 May, 1885.
CLARK SWALLOW	East Bridge-water.	31 December, 1886.
GEORGE WARREN HAMMOND . . .	Boston.	

2 February, 1876.

EDWIN SHEPARD BARRETT	Concord.	
CHARLES VOSE BEMIS, A.B., M.D.	Medford . .	31 December, 1883.
JOSHUA PETER BODFISH (Rev.) . .	Boston.	
CHARLES WELLS HUBBARD, A.B. .	Weston.	
FRED TEBBETS	Milford . .	31 December, 1880.

1 March, 1876.

JAMES FREEMAN DANA GARFIELD .	Fitchburg . .	Life Member, 1878.
ALEXANDER SYLVANUS PORTER . .	Boston.	
SAMUEL HAMMOND RUSSELL . . .	Boston.	
GEORGE THOMPSON WIGGIN, S.B. .	Hyde Park .	31 December, 1883.
GEORGE HAYWARD ALLAN . . .	New York, N.Y.	Died 15 March, 1886.

5 April, 1876.

HERBERT SHAW CARRUTH, S.B. .	Dorchester.	
RUFUS GEORGE FREDERICK CANDAGE	Brookline.	
EUGENE FRANCIS ENDICOTT . . .	Chelsea . .	Resgd. 17 February, 1887
CHRISTOPHER AMORY HACK . . .	Taunton . .	Life Member, 1877.

3 May, 1876.

FRANCIS HENRY MANNING	Boston . . .	Life Member, 1876.
JOHN FARWELL ANDERSON . . .	Portland, Me.	Died 25 December, 1887.
STEPHEN MINOT PITMAN, Ph.B., M.E.	Cambridge .	31 December, 1880.

8

7 June, 1876.

NAME.	RESIDENCE.	MEMBERSHIP CEASED.
FREDERIC RUSSELL NOURSE, A.B.	Boston. .	Disappeared in London, Eng., 3 March, 1886.
JOSEPH BURNETT	Boston. . .	Life Member, 1884.
CHARLES RUSSELL TRAIN, A.M.	Boston. . .	Died 29 July, 1885.
JOHN WEISS (Rev.), A.M. . . .	Boston. . .	Resigned 15 March, 1877.

6 September, 1876.

JOHN BEAR DOANE COGSWELL, A.B., LL.B.	Yarmouth. .	31 December, 1880.
SIMON WILLIAM HATHEWAY, A.M. .	Dedham .	Resgd. 27 February, 1888.
FREDERIC LEWIS GAY	Cambridge .	31 December, 1884.
CHARLES WELLS HAYES, A.M., D.D.	Portland, Me.	Elected Corresponding Member, 7 September, 1881.

4 October, 1876.

STEPHEN HOBBS HAYES (Rev.), A.B.	Boston. . .	31 December, 1882.

1 November, 1876.

ARMAND GÜŸZ	Boston. . .	Resigned 23 June, 1880.

6 December, 1876.

CHARLES PELHAM GREENOUGH, A.B., LL.B.	Boston.
JOSEPH HEBER SMITH, M.D. . . .	Melrose.
GEORGE AUGUSTUS GORDON, A.M.	Lowell.

5 January, 1877.

HENRY DEERING	Portland, Me.	
GEORGE SHATTUCK CUSHING . . .	Boston.	
JOHN WILLIAM LEATHERBEE . . .	Boston. . .	31 December, 1888.
WILLIAM HENRY EMERY	Boston.	
BENNETT FRANKLIN DAVENPORT, A.M., M.D.	Boston.	
CARROLL DAVIDSON WRIGHT, A.M.	Reading.	

7 February, 1877.

JOHN GOULD ANTHONY	Cambridge .	Died 16 October, 1877.
EDWARD PRESTON USHER, A.M., LL.B.	Lynn . . .	Life Member, 1877.
SAMUEL WALLACE WINSLOW . . .	Boston.	

7 March, 1877.

NAME.	RESIDENCE.	MEMBERSHIP CEASED.
RICHARD WILLARD SEARS . . .	. Boston . . .	Died 14 September, 1880.

4 April, 1877.

WILLARD SPENCER ALLEN, A. M.	. Boston.	
CRANMORE NESMITH WALLACE .	Braintree.	

2 May, 1877.

FRANKLIN STILES PHELPS	Lynn . .	Life Member, 1877.
LEONARD THOMPSON, Jr.	Woburn . .	Life Member, 1877.
FRANCIS HENRY NICHOLS	Boston . . .	1 July, 1891.
CHARLES HENRY JAMES DOUGLAS, A. B.	Providence, R.I.	Resgd. 5 September, 1881.

5 September, 1877.

EDWIN FORBES WATERS	Newton . .	Life Member, 1877.
JOHN SIMPSON EMERY	Boston.	
BENJAMIN OSGOOD PEIRCE, A. B.	Cambridge .	Died 12 November, 1883.
FRANCIS MARION BOUTWELL . . .	Groton.	
CHARLES FURNEAUX	Melrose . .	31 December, 1882.

3 October, 1877.

FREDERIC HENRY VIAUX, A.B. . .	Boston . . .	Resigned, 1882.
CHARLES HENRY MILLER, Jr. . .	Boston . . .	Resgd. 23 November, 1891.

7 November, 1877.

CHARLES GRANVILLE WAY . . .	Boston . .	Life Member, 1877.

5 December, 1877.

GEORGE HENRY SNELLING, A.M. .	Boston . . .	Died 18 January, 1892.
WILLIAM WILKINS WARREN . . .	Boston . . .	Life Member, 1884. Died 23 January, 1890.

2 January, 1878.

BEZA LINCOLN	Boston . . .	Life Member, 1877.
ANDREW DIMOCK	Boston.	

6 February, 1878.

THOMAS SHERWIN, A.B.	Boston.	
FREDERICK CLIFTON PIERCE . . .	Barre . . .	31 December, 1884.
WILLIAM HENRY SAWTELL . . .	Boston . . .	31 December, 1886.
SILAS KETCHAM (Rev.)	Windsor, Conn.	Died 24 April, 1880.
MOSES KIMBALL	Boston.	

NAME.	RESIDENCE.	MEMBERSHIP CEASED.
SIDNEY PERLEY, LL. B.	Boxford.	
FREDERICK JACKSON	Newton	Resgd. 20 January, 1882.

6 March, 1878.

HENRY CORNELIUS HAYDEN	Newton	31 December, 1888.
HENRY FRANCIS DOUGLAS	Providence, R. I.	Resgd. 5 September, 1881.
JAMES WILLARD PRESTON, A. M.	Boston.	31 December, 1886.

3 April, 1878.

DANIEL BODWELL WHITTIER	Boston.	31 December, 1882.
DUDLEY FOSTER	Billerica.	

1 May, 1878.

FRANCIS HENRY SWAN, A. M.	Charlestown.	Resgd. 27 December, 1889.
PEARCE WENTWORTH PENHALLOW.	Boston.	Died 9 December, 1885.
FREDERIC BEECH PIERCE	Dorchester.	1 October, 1890.
EDWARD WINSLOW	Boston.	Died 26 May, 1883.

5 June, 1878.

STEPHEN DECATUR SALMON, Jr.	Boston.	Resigned 1884.
JAMES SHEPHARD PIKE	Calais, Me.	Died 29 November, 1882.
GEORGE WASHINGTON KELLY (Rev.)	Haverhill.	
JAMES ALBERT EDGERLY	Great Falls, N. H.	
ALBERT KENDALL TEELE, A. B., D. D.	Milton.	
STANTON BLAKE, A. B.	Boston.	Life Member, 1878. Died 21 April, 1889.
JOHN HENRY HARDY, A. B.	Arlington.	Resgd. 31 December, 1889.

4 September, 1878.

ISAAC CHAUNCEY WYMAN, A.M.,LL.B.	Salem.	
GEORGE KUHN CLARKE, LL. B.	Needham.	Life Member, 1883.
THOMAS EDWARD BARTLETT	Worcester.	31 December, 1885.
GEORGE WASHINGTON GAY, M. D.	Boston.	1 July, 1891.
WILLIAM AUGUSTUS MOWRY, A. M., Ph. D.	Providence, R.I.	

2 October, 1878.

THOMAS LUCINDUS ROGERS, A. B.	Newton	31 December, 1888.
LUTHER CLARK, A. B., M. D.	Boston.	Life Member, 1878. Died 26 September, 1884.

6 November, 1878.

Name.	Residence.	Membership ceased.
Frank Warren Hackett, A. M.	Portsmouth, N. H.	
William Francis Crafts . . .	Boston.	
Anson Titus, Jr. (Rev.)	Weymouth	Life Member, 1887.

4 December, 1878.

Samuel Kidder	Lowell.	
Charles Merrick Gay, A. B. . .	Newton.	
William Ellis Endicott	Canton. . .	Resigned 15 June, 1889.
Gyles Merrill	Haverhill.	

1 January, 1879.

Edward Naman Sheppard, A. B. .	New Haven, Conn.	31 December, 1885.
Grenville Howland Norcross, A. B., LL. B.	Boston .	Life Member, 1885.
Augustine Jones, A. M., LL. B. .	Lynn.	
Ira Leavitt Sanderson, M. D. . .	Jersey City, N. J.	Life Member, 1879.

5 February, 1879.

Robert Maurice Bailey, Jr. . .	Boston.	
Francis Nicoll Zabriskie, D. D. .	Quincy . .	Resigned, 1879.
William Henry Wardwell . . .	Newton.	
Josiah Hayden Drummond, A. M., LL. D.	Portland, Me.	31 December, 1882.
George Zabriskie Gray, A. M., D. D.	Cambridge .	Resigned 2 January, 1887.
Alfred Henry Hersey	Hingham.	
Albert Alonzo Folsom	Boston.	

5 March, 1879.

Amos Josiah Boyden, S. B. . . .	Foxborough .	31 December, 1887.
William Barrows, A. B., D. D. .	Reading . .	Resgd. 22 January, 1890.
William Augustus Bowdlear . .	Boston.	

2 April, 1879.

Arthur Codman [1]	Bristol, R. I.	
William Henry Allen	Boston.	

7 May, 1879.

James Morison, A. M., M. D. . .	Quincy . . .	Died 20 May, 1882.
William Henry Odiorne	Cambridge .	Resigned, 1884.

[1] Mr. Codman now (1892) writes his name Arthur Amory Codman.

NAME.	RESIDENCE.	MEMBERSHIP CEASED.
HENRY EDWIN FALES	Milford . .	31 December, 1882.
GEORGE AUGUSTUS PERKINS, M.D.	Salem . . .	Resgd.31 December, 1891.
DAVID MOORE BALCH, S.B. . . .	Salem . . .	31 December, 1882.

4 June, 1879.

GEORGE FREDERICK GRAY	Dover, N.H.	Died 6 March, 1880.
JOSEPH WILLARD BROWN, A.M. .	Medford . .	31 December, 1883.

3 September, 1879.

JOHN WHITTEMORE FARWELL . .	Melrose.	
ASA PORTER MORSE	Cambridge .	Fees commuted, 1889.
EPHRAIM ORCUTT JAMESON (Rev.), A.B.	Medway.	
SAMUEL SNOW, Ph.B., LL.B.	Cambridge.	

1 October, 1879.

DANA BOARDMAN PUTNAM, A.M., M.D.	Boston . . .	Died 11 February, 1881.
FREDERIC GREGORY FORSYTH . . .	Portland, Me.	31 December, 1883.

5 November, 1879.

BENJAMIN BRADLEY	Boston . . .	31 December, 1884.
CHARLES BAILEY GOOKIN	Boston.	
ROYAL WOODWARD . . .	Albany, N.Y.	Life Member, 1879. Died 2 October, 1882.
WILLIAM EATON FOSTER, A.M. . .	Providence, R.I.	

3 December, 1879.

JOHN DANDRIDGE HENLEY LUCE .	Boston . . .	Resgd. 5 January, 1882.
JONATHAN EDWARDS, A.B., M.D. .	New Haven, Conn.	Life Member, 1879. Died 19 June, 1886.
FREDERICK FANNING AYER, A.B.	Lowell.	
LUTHER FARNHAM (Rev.). A.M. .	Boston . . .	See 3 November, 1853. Life Member, 1879.

7 January, 1880.

ALPHONSO JEROME ROBINSON. A.M.	Boston . . .	Died 24 April, 1889.
ROBERT FRANKLIN PENNELL. A.B. .	Exeter, N.H.	31 December, 1883.
JOHN LORD HAYES. A.M., LL.D. .	Cambridge .	Died 18 April, 1887.
WALTER ELIOT THWING	Jamaica Plain	Life Member, 1880.
FRANCIS FAULKNER EMERY .	Boston . . .	Life Member, 1882.

4 February, 1880.

NAME.	RESIDENCE.	MEMBERSHIP CEASED.
EDWARD PENNIMAN BLISS, A. M.	Boston . . .	Resgd. 24 February, 1883.

3 March, 1880.

JOSEPH NASH	Boston . . .	31 December, 1884.
WESTON LEWIS	Boston . . .	Resgd. 5 February, 1885.
ALFRED OTIS LARKIN	Portsmouth, N. H.	
OBADIAH BROWN HADWEN . . .	Worcester.	

7 April, 1880.

CHARLES EDWARD HOSMER, A. B., M. D.	Billerica . .	31 December, 1883.
HORACE FAIRBANKS	St. Johnsbury, Vt.	Died 17 March, 1888.
SAMUEL JUNE BARROWS, D. B. . .	Dorchester.	
JOHN SAMUEL WHITING, A.B., M.D.	Charlestown .	31 December, 1887.
OLIVER RICHARDSON CLARK . .	Tewksbury .	Died 5 March, 1887.
WILLIAM SMITH TILDEN	Medfield.	

5 May, 1880.

WILLIAM EBEN STONE, A.B. . . .	Cambridge.	
SAMUEL EDWARD WARREN, C. E. .	Newton.	
HENRY ERNEST WOODS	Boston.	
CALVIN TILDEN PHILLIPS . . .	Hanover . .	Life Member, 1885. Died 15 January, 1892.
JOSEPH BENJAMIN MOORS . . .	Boston . . .	Resigned 12 April, 1884.

2 June, 1880.

FREDERIC LORD RICHARDSON . . .	Boston.	
CHARLES ALVAN ROGERS	Boston . . .	Resigned 9 July, 1890.

1 September, 1880.

ELIJAH FRANKLIN HOWE (Rev.), A. B.	Newton . .	Resgd. 16 January, 1883.
ALONZO BOND WENTWORTH, LL. B.	Dedham . .	1 July, 1891.
GEORGE EUGENE BELKNAP, U. S. N.	Malden.	
JEREMIAH CHAPMAN KITTREDGE . .	Tewksbury.	
RUSSELL ARNOLD BALLOU	Boston . . .	31 December, 1883.

6 October, 1880.

JOSEPH FENNELLY BALLISTER . . .	Newton.	
CHARLES HENRY BASS BRECK . .	Boston.	

3 November, 1880.

Name.	Residence	Membership ceased.
John Davis Long, A.B., LL.D.	Hingham	31 December, 1888.

1 December, 1880.

Charles Ronello Elder	Boston	Resgd. 6 January, 1886.
John Henry Barrows (Rev.)	Boston	31 December, 1882.
William Jay Pettigrew, A.M.	Boston	31 December, 1882.
Paul Ansel Chadbourne, A.M., M.D., D.D., LL.D.	Williamstown	Died 23 February, 1883.

5 January, 1881.

John Orne Green, A.M., M.D.	Boston.	
Timothy Bigelow, A.M.	Boston	31 December, 1883.
Henry Franklin Mills	Boston	Died 7 December, 1888.
Henry Sturgis Russell, A.B.	Milton	Resgd. 1 January, 1889.
Frederick Lothrop Ames, A.B.	Easton	Life Member, 1885.
John Howard Burdakin	Dedham.	
Henry Augustus Church	Boston.	
Richard Ingalls Attwill	Boston.	

2 February, 1881.

Clement Willis	Boston	Died 20 June, 1889.
Charles William Parsons, A.M., M.D.	Providence, R.I.	
George Sumner Mann	Boston	Life Member, 1881.
Charles Carroll Dawson, LL.B.	Lowell	1 July, 1891.

2 March, 1881.

William Ellery Bright	Waltham	Died 12 March, 1882.
Fritz Hermann Jordan	Portland, Me.	
Albert St. John Chambré, D.D.	Lowell.	
William Peirce	Boston	31 December, 1883.
Curtis Guild	Boston	Life Member, 1881.
Charles Augustus Jones	Boston	See 3 July, 1867. Life Member, 1881. Died 10 April, 1884.
Henry Allen Cooke (Rev.)	Boston	6 November, 1889.

6 April, 1881.

David Boardman Flint	Watertown	Life Member, 1881.
Samuel Tucker Bent	Milton	Died 2 November, 1885.
Charles Pickering Bowditch, A.M.	Boston	Life Member, 1881.
Waldo Thompson	Swampscott	Life Member, 1881.

DON GLEASON HILL, LL. B. . . . Dedham.
WALTER HAMLET FAUNCE . . . Kingston.
CHARLES CROSBY WILLIAMS, M. D. Boston.

4 May, 1881.

ROYAL OTIS STORRS . . . . . . Dedham . . Resgd. 15 October, 1883.
RALPH WOOD KENYON, D. B., A. M. Cambridge . Elected Corresponding
                                            Member, 4 January,
                                            1882.
JOSIAH DRAKE . . . . Cincinnati, Ohio Died 24 December, 1887.
WILLIAM SPOONER SMITH (Rev.), A.B. Newton.
JOHN McNAB CURRIER, M. D. . . Castleton, Vt. 31 December, 1886.

1 June, 1881.

FREEBORN FAIRFIELD RAYMOND, 2d Newton.
GEORGE MORGAN BROWNE, A. B. . Boston.

7 September, 1881.

HORATIO GATES SANFORD . . . . Gloucester . 31 December, 1886.
JOHN WOODBRIDGE DICKINSON, A.M. Boston . . . 31 December, 1884.
CHARLES ALEXANDER NELSON, A.M. Somerville . 31 December, 1887.
WATERMAN STONE . . . . . Providence, R.I. Life Member, 1883.
HERBERT BAXTER ADAMS, A.M., Ph.D. Baltimore, Md. Resigned, 1886.

2 November, 1881.

NAHUM CAPEN, LL. D. . . . . . Boston . . . Died 8 January, 1886.
DAVID JILLSON . . . . Attleborough . Life Member, 1882. Died
                                            30 July, 1889.
EGBERT COFFIN SMYTH, A. M., D.D. Andover.
JOHN GERRISH WEBSTER . . . . Boston . . . Died 7 February, 1886.

7 December, 1881.

RALPH WILLARD ALLEN, D. D. . . Malden . . Died 16 April, 1891.
JOSHUA MONTGOMERY SEARS, A. B. . Boston . . . Life Member, 1881.
WILLIAM GRAY WISE . . . . . Auburn, N. Y. See 7 April, 1858.
                                            Died 13 Septem'r, 1886.
GEORGE PLUMER SMITH . . . . Philadelphia, Pa. Life Member, 1881.
GEORGE ALEXANDER OVIATT (Rev.), Sudbury . . Died 1 June, 1887.
   A. M.
CHARLES ALFRED WELCH, A. B. . Boston . . . Life Member, 1881.
GEORGE BAXTER HYDE, A. M. . . Boston . . . Life Member, 1882. Died
                                            8 July, 1889.

9

4 January, 1882.

NAME.	RESIDENCE.	MEMBERSHIP CEASED.
WILLIAM EDWARD COFFIN . . .	Richmond, Ind.	
GEORGE ANSON JACKSON (Rev.), Ph. B., A. M.	Swampscott .	Life Member, 1883.
GILBERT NASH . .	Weymouth .	Died 13 April, 1888.

1 February, 1882.

SAMUEL HOPKINS EMERY, A.M., D.D.	Taunton . .	See Corresponding Roll, 7 November, 1855.
CHARLES WOODBURY STEVENS . .	Boston.	
EDMUND JANES CLEVELAND . . .	Elizabeth, N.J.	Life Member, 1882.
GEORGE EMERY LITTLEFIELD, A.B.	Somerville.	
BYRON WESTON, A. M.	Dalton.	
NEWTON TALBOT	Boston.	
FRANK MORTON AMES	Canton.	
ROLAND WORTHINGTON	Boston.	
HENRY PICKERING WALCOTT, A.B., M.D.	Cambridge.	

1 March, 1882.

HENRY MORRIS, A.M., LL.D. . .	Springfield .	Resgd. 13 January, 1885.
JAMES BOURNE AYER, A.M., M.D.	Boston.	
ALFRED CUSHING HERSEY	Hingham . .	Died 8 March, 1888.
CHARLES EMERY STEVENS, A.B. .	Worcester .	31 December, 1888.

5 April, 1882.

STEPHEN SALISBURY, A.M., LL.D.	Worcester	Life Member, 1882. Died 24 August, 1884.
ROBERT ROBERTS BISHOP, A.M., LL.B.	Newton.	
JAMES PHINNEY BAXTER, A.M. . .	Portland, Me.	
DAVID BRAINARD WESTON . .	Charlestown.	

3 May, 1882.

SAMUEL LELAND MONTAGUE . . .	Cambridge.	
EZRA CONANT	Boston . . .	Life Member, 1883. Died 20 October, 1888.
EDWARD HARTWELL KIDDER, A.M.	Brooklyn, N.Y.	Life Member, 1882.
EDWIN TEMPLE HORNE, A.M. .	Boston . .	31 December, 1885.

7 June, 1882.

AI BAKER THOMPSON, A.M. . . .	Concord, N.H.	Died 12 September, 1890.
CALEB BENJAMIN TILLINGHAST . .	Boston.	

6 September, 1882.

Name.	Residence.	Membership ceased.
Edward Doubleday Harris	Brooklyn, N. Y.	Life Member, 1882.
George Knowles Snow	Watertown	Died 3 August, 1885.
Charles Larned	Boston	Life Member, 1882.
Thomas Lincoln Casey, U.S.A.	Washington, D.C.	
Daniel Rollins (Rev.)	Boston.	
William Pitt Robinson	Somerville.	
Charles Laforest Alden	Hyde Park	31 December, 1887.
John William Bell, LL.B.	Boston	1 July, 1891.

4 October, 1882.

Edward Phelps Lull, U.S.N., A.M.	Charlestown	31 December, 1886.

1 November, 1882.

Seth Alonzo Ranlett	Newton	Life Member, 1882.
Wallace Henry Montague	Kansas City, Mo.	6 November, 1889.
Charles Frederic Farlow	Newton	Life Member, 1886.
Edward James Young, A.M., D.D.	Cambridge.	
Augustus Russ, A.M.	Boston.	

6 December, 1882.

Fred Hovey Allen (Rev.)	Boston	31 December, 1887.
Horatio Davis	Boston.	
Samuel Hall	Brookline	Resgd. 11 December, 1891.

3 January, 1883.

John Kimball Rogers	Brookline	See 6 October, 1858. Died 27 January, 1888.
John Murray Forbes	Milton	Life Member, 1883.
Henry Russell Shaw, A.B.	Boston.	
Oliver Ames	Easton	Life Member, 1883.
Andrew Preston Peabody, A.M., D.D., LL.D.	Cambridge.	
Benjamin Hill Dewing	Revere	Life Member, 1884. Died 28 September, 1890.
Camillus George Kidder, A.B., LL.B.	Orange, N.J.	Life Member, 1883.
Shebnah Rich	Boston.	
Edward Stanwood, A.M.	Brookline.	
Joshua Foster Ober, A.M.	Newton	1 October, 1890.
James Robinson Newhall	Lynn.	

NAME.	RESIDENCE.	MEMBERSHIP CEASED
GEORGE SEWALL BOUTWELL. LL.D.	Groton.	
WILLIAM EATON CHANDLER, A.M., LL.B.	Concord, N.H.	
FRANCIS ORMOND FRENCH, A.B., LL.B.	New York, N.Y.	
JOHN MILTON FESSENDEN, A.M.	Princeton, N.J.	Died 8 February, 1883.
EDWARD ALBERT KELLY, A.M..	Boston.	
CHARLES CHAUNCEY, A.B.	Philadelphia, Pa.	
HORACE STUART CUMMINGS, A.B.	Exeter, N.H.	
JEROME HENRY KIDDER, U.S.N., A.M., M.D.	Washington, D.C.	Life Member, 1883. Died 8 April, 1889.
JAMES SULLIVAN AMORY, A.M..	Boston.	Died 8 June, 1884.

7 February, 1883.

CHARLES AUGUSTUS SAYWARD	Ipswich	31 December, 1887.
OAKES ANGIER AMES	Easton.	Life Member, 1883.
ALBERT PALMER, A.M.	Boston.	31 December, 1885.
FRANCIS HENSHAW DEWEY, A.M., LL.B., LL.D.	Worcester.	Died 16 December, 1887.
ROBERT KENDALL DARRAH	Boston.	Died 22 May, 1885.
JOSEPH PINCKNEY PONSONBY BISHOP	Taunton	31 December, 1886.
STILLMAN BAXTER PRATT	Marlborough.	1 October, 1890.
GEORGE CHEYNE SHATTUCK, A.M., M.D.	Boston.	

7 March, 1883.

WILLIAM LADD CHAFFIN (Rev.)	Easton.	Resgd. 12 January, 1892.
WILLIAM COPLEY WINSLOW, A.M., Ph.D., Sc.D., L.H.D., D.D., D.C.L., LL.D.	Boston.	
JEFFREY RICHARDSON BRACKETT, A.B.	Quincy	Resgd. 10 January, 1890.
JONATHAN EASTMAN PECKER, S.B.	Concord, N.H.	

4 April, 1883.

HORACE DAVIS, A.B., LL.D.	San Francisco, Cal.	Life Member. 1883.
WALDO HIGGINSON, A.M.	Boston	See 3 September, 1845.
SAMUEL PEARCE MAY	Newton.	
CHARLES FRANCIS CONANT.	Cambridge	Died 26 July, 1886.
EDWARD STEARNS	Lincoln	Died 20 June, 1891.
AMOS HADLEY, A.M., Ph.D.	Concord, N.H.	

2 May, 1883.

JOHN AUGUSTUS POOR	Roxbury	Resigned January, 1889.
AARON DAVIS WELD FRENCH	Boston	Life Member, 1883.

Name.	Residence.	Membership ceased.
John Davis Williams French, A.B.	Boston . . .	Life Member, 1883.
Henry Griswold Jesup (Rev.), A.M.	Hanover, N.H.	
Silas Reed, M.D.	Boston . . .	Died 1 October, 1886.

5 June, 1883.

Eugene Bigelow Hagar, A.M., LL.B.	Boston . . .	Resigned 1886. Re-elected 5 November, 1890.
Francis Amasa Walker, A.M., Ph.D., LL.D.	Boston.	

5 September, 1883.

George Sheffield, LL.B. . . .	Cambridge .	Died 30 December, 1884.
Sereno Brainard Pratt	Boston.	
Edward Ashton Rollins, A.M. .	Philadelphia, Pa.	Life Member, 1884. Died 7 September, 1885.
George Mooar, A.M., D.D. . .	Oakland, Cal.	

3 October, 1883.

Frederick Milton Ballou . . .	Providence, R.I.	Died 4 May, 1889.
Ephraim Williams Allen (Rev.), A.B.	Taunton . .	See 3 October, 1866. Resgd. 31 Dec., 1888.
Thomas Hamilton Murray . . .	Brookline . .	31 December, 1887.

7 November, 1883.

Frank Eliot Bradish, A.B. . .	Cambridge.	
William Lee, M.D.	Washington, D.C.	
William Evarts Field	Newton.	

5 December, 1883.

George Willis Cooke (Rev.) . .	Dedham . .	31 December, 1886.
Henry Wilder Foote (Rev.), A.M.	Boston . . .	Died 30 May, 1889.
Charles Acton Drew, A.B., LL.B.	Newton . .	Resgd. 17 September, 1890.
John Harvey Treat, A.M. . . .	Lawrence.	
John Lindsay Stevenson . . .	Boston . . .	Resgd. 23 February, 1888.

2 January, 1884.

Timothy Thompson Sawyer . . .	Charlestown.

6 February, 1884.

James Adams Woolson	Cambridge .	Life Member, 1884.
Alonzo Ames Miner, A.M., D.D., LL.D.	Boston.	
Leopold Morse	Boston.	

NAME.	RESIDENCE.	MEMBERSHIP CEASED.
MARSHALL MUNROE CUTTER (Rev.), A.M.	Malden.	
FRANK BROWNELL	Newton . .	31 December, 1886.
HARRY CLAY BROWNELL	Newton . .	31 December, 1886.
JAMES JUNIUS GOODWIN . . .	Hartford, Conn.	Life Member, 1884.

5 March, 1884.

JAMES FRANCIS DORSEY	Newton . .	Resigned April, 1889.
FRANCIS FESSENDEN, A.B. . . .	Portland, Me.	
JACOB WARREN MANNING	Reading.	
EDWARD ELLERTON PRATT, A.B., LL.B.	Boston . . .	Life Member, 1884.
JAMES JOHN HOWARD GREGORY, A.M.	Marblehead .	Resgd. 13 February, 1892.

2 April, 1884.

NATHAN MATTHEWS, Jr., A.B. . .	Boston.	
CHARLES ADDISON RICHARDSON, A.M.	Chelsea . .	Died 18 January, 1891.
CHARLES FRANCIS POTTER	Boston.	
ABIJAH THOMPSON	Winchester .	Life Member, 1884.
SAMUEL FRANKLIN HAM, D.M.D. .	Boston . . .	Resigned January, 1888.
ABIJAH PERKINS MARVIN (Rev.), A.M.	Lancaster . .	Died 19 October, 1889.

7 May, 1884.

GARDNER ASAPH CHURCHILL . . .	Boston.	
WARREN LADD	New Bedford.	
ISAAC STORY	Somerville.	

4 June, 1884.

ALBERT LORENZO EASTMAN . . .	Hampstead . N.H.	Died 12 January, 1891.
THOMAS JACKSON LOTHROP, A.B. .	Taunton.	
SIDNEY HOMER BUTTRICK	Melrose . .	1 October, 1890.

3 September, 1884.

JAMES MASCARENE HUBBARD (Rev.), A.B.	Boston.	
FRANK FARNSWORTH STARR . . .	Middletown, Conn.	Life Member, 1884.

1 October, 1884.

THOMAS WESTON, Jr., A.M. . . .	Newton. . .	1 July, 1891.
GEORGE CALVIN CODMAN	Deering, Me.	Resgd. 26 December, 1888.
FRANCIS FLINT FORSAITH.[1] A.B., M.D.	Weymouth .	Resigned 9 July, 1890.

[1] Dr Forsaith now (1891) writes his name "Forsyth."

5 November, 1884.

Name.	Residence.	Membership ceased.
William Henry Rollins, A. M.	Portsmouth, N. H.	
George Potter Barrett	Portland. Me.	Life Member, 1884.
Rowland Ellis	Newton.	

3 December, 1884.

John Nicholas Brown	Providence, R.I.	Life Member, 1884.
George Moulton Adams, A. M., D. D.	Holliston.	

7 January, 1885.

James Farrington Pickering	Charlestown.	
Jerome Fenelon Manning	Lowell	6 November, 1889.
Jonas Gilman Clark	Worcester.	
Waldo Burnett (Rev.), A. M.	Southborough	Life Member, 1885.
Levi Lincoln Willcutt	Boston	Life Member, 1885.
Nathaniel Thayer, A. B.	Boston	Life Member, 1885.
Myles Standish, A. M., M. D.	Boston.	
Benjamin Cutler Hardwick	Boston	Life Member, 1885.
Arthur Welland Blake	Brookline	Life Member, 1885.
Charles Louis Flint, Jr., S. B.	Boston	Life Member, 1885.
Edmund Sanford Clark, A. M.	Boston	Life Member, 1885.
James William Clarke, A. M.	Dorchester	Life Member, 1885.
Arthur March Pius Clark[1] (Rev.), A. B.	New York, N.Y.	Life Member, 1885.
Henry Oscar Houghton, A. M.	Cambridge	Life Member, 1885.
Richard Sullivan	Boston.	
Charles Carroll Carpenter (Rev.), A. M.	Mt. Vernon, N. H.	
Ezra Farnsworth, Jr.	Boston	Life Member, 1885.
Arthur Gregory Richardson	Boston	Life Member, 1885.
Daniel Berkeley Updike	Boston	Resgd. 12 December, 1889.

4 February, 1885.

Joseph Mason, A. M.	Worcester.	
Edward Newman Packard, A. M., D. D.	Dorchester	Life Member, 1885.
Frederick Hastings Rindge, A. B.	Cambridge	Life Member, 1885.
James Sidney Allen	East Bridgewater.	
Andrew Coatsworth Fearing, Jr.	Boston	Fees commuted, 1891.

[1] Mr. Clark, in writing his name, now (1891) omits " Pius."

4 March, 1885.

NAME.	RESIDENCE.	MEMBERSHIP CEASED.
GEORGE FRANKLIN PUTNAM . . .	Boston.	
GEORGE THEODORE CRUFT . . .	Bethlehem, N. H.	

1 April, 1885.

JOHN CLARK GILBERT . . . . . Boston.
WALTER ADAMS, A. B. . . . . . Framingham . Life Member, 1885.
FRANK GRAY CLARK (Rev.), A. M. . Gloucester.
MOSES JONES WENTWORTH, A. M., Chicago, Ill. . Life Member, 1885.
LL. B.
LYMAN WILLARD DENSMORE . . . Hillsborough, N. H.
OLIVER LEONARD BRIGGS . . . . Boston.

6 May, 1885.

HENRY CABOT LODGE, A. B., LL. B., Nahant.
Ph. D.

3 June, 1885.

EDWARD BOUTELLE BLASLAND . . Boston.

2 September, 1885.

ELIHU CHAUNCEY, A. M. . . . . . New York, N.Y. Life Member, 1885.
BENJAMIN APTHORP GOULD, A.M., Cambridge . Fees commuted, 1890.
Ph. D., LL. D.
DANIEL WELD BAKER . . . . . . Boston . . . 1 July, 1891.

7 October, 1885.

WILLIAM WALLACE BAILEY, A. B., Nashua, N. H.
LL. B.

4 November, 1885.

CARLTON ALBERT STAPLES (Rev.) . Lexington.
BENJAMIN CUTLER CLARK, A. B. . . Boston.

2 December, 1885.

GEORGE JARVIS PRESCOTT, A. M., Boston.
D. B.
HENRY HASTINGS KIMBALL, A. B. . Boston . . . 1 October, 1890.
HENRY AINSWORTH PARKER (Rev.), Cambridge.
A. M.
EDGAR WOOD UPTON . . . . . . Peabody . . . 1 July. 1891.

6 January, 1886.

Name.	Residence.	Membership ceased.
Warren Hapgood	Boston.	
Nathan Allen, A.M., M.D., LL.D.	Lowell . . .	See 5 May, 1858.
		Died 1 January, 1889.
Lyman Dewey Stevens, A.M. . .	Nashua, N.H.	Resgd. 7 October, 1889.
Hezekiah Spencer Sheldon . .	Suffield, Conn.	Life Member, 1886.
Bradford Morton Fullerton, A.B., D.D.	Waltham.	

3 February, 1886.

James Schouler, A.B. . . .	Boston.	
William Green Shillaber . . .	Boston . . .	Life Member, 1886.
George Eben Thompson, S.B., M.D.	Boston.	
Harry Fairfield Hamilton, S.B., D.M.D.	Boston . . .	Life Member, 1887.

3 March, 1886.

Thomas Goddard Frothingham .	Charlestown .	Life Member, 1886.
Thomas Emerson Proctor . . .	Boston . . .	Life Member, 1886.
Charles Upham Bell, A.M. . .	Lawrence . .	1 July, 1891.
Edwin Perry Wells, S.B. . . .	Somerville.	

7 April, 1886.

Edward Lillie Pierce, A.B., LL.B., LL.D.	Milton . .	Resgd. 5 October, 1889.
Charles Harrison Littlefield .	Lawrence.	
William Francis Wheeler . .	Lincoln .	Died 10 October, 1890.
Charles Hicks Saunders . . .	Cambridge.	
Charles William Galloupe . .	Beverly . .	Life Member, 1886.
Robert Charles Winthrop,Jr.,A.M.	Boston . . .	Life Member, 1886.

5 May, 1886.

William Stanford Stevens, A.M., M.D.	Boston.	
George Frisbie Hoar, A.B., LL.B., LL.D.	Worcester.	

2 June, 1886.

Pliny Earle, A.M., M.D. . . .	Northampton .	Life Member, 1888.
		Died 17 May, 1892.

1 September, 1886.

Charles Henry Adams	Boston.	

6 October, 1886.

William Tracy Eustis	Boston.	
Eben Putnam	Cambridge .	Life Member, 1886.

3 November, 1886.

NAME.	RESIDENCE.	MEMBERSHIP CEASED.
GEORGE AUGUSTUS KENDALL . . .	Walpole.	
RAPHAEL PUMPELLY	Newport, R. I.	

1 December, 1886.

WILLIAM ELLIOT GRIFFIS, A.M., D.D. Boston.

5 January, 1887.

COUNT EDGAR DE VALCOURT-VERMONT, LL.M.	Tivoli, N.Y. . .	6 November, 1889.
JAMES HENRY STARK	Boston.	
JAMES EDWARD RADFORD HILL . .	Boston . . .	Life Member, 1887.
EDWARD BAKER WILDER	Dorchester .	Life Member, 1887.

2 February, 1887.

NATHANIEL LEECH HOOPER, A.M., LL.B.	Boston . . .	Resigned 3 July, 1890.
WILLIAM HENRY UPTON, A.B., LL.B., LL.M.	Walla Walla, Washington.	
LUCIUS BOLLES MARSH	Boston.	
CHAUNCEY REA BURR, Ph.B., M.D.	Portland, Me.	
CHARLES EVERETT RANLETT . . .	Newton.	
EDWARD HENRY WILLIAMS . . .	Jamaica Plain	Life Member, 1887.

2 March, 1887.

STEPHEN PASCHALL SHARPLES, S.B.	Cambridge.	
LEANDER THOMPSON (Rev.), A.M. .	Woburn . .	Fees commuted, 1890.
GEORGE BAILEY LORING, A.B., M.D.	Salem . . .	Died 14 September, 1891.
FRANKLIN LEONARD POPE	Elizabeth, N.J.	
WILLIAM INGALLS MONROE, A.B., LL.B.	Boston.	
WILLIAM ALLEN HAYES. 2d, A.M., LL.B.	Cambridge .	1 October, 1890.

6 April, 1887.

CHARLES HENRY POPE (Rev.), A.B.	Farmington, Me.	
JOHN RITCHIE, Jr.	Boston.	
WILLIAM SWEETSER HEYWOOD (Rev.)	Boston.	
WILLIAM WARD WIGHT, A.M. . .	Milwaukee, Wis.	Life Member, 1887.
JOHN DENNISON KINGSBURY, A.M., D.D.	Bradford.	
BENJAMIN CUSHING, A.B., M.D. .	Dorchester.	

4 May, 1887.

Name.	Residence.	Membership ceased.
WILLIAM LAWRENCE, A.B., D.D.	Cambridge	Life Member, 1887.
ARTHUR WENTWORTH HAMILTON EATON (Rev.), A.B.	Boston.	

1 June, 1887.

WILLIAM DUMMER NORTHEND, A.M.	Salem	1 October, 1890.
WILLIAM HENRY KENNARD	Boston	Died 6 July, 1891.
WILLIAM FRANCIS HARBACH	Newton.	
ROBERT MARION PRATT	Boston.	
EDWARD TOBEY TUCKER, A.B., M.D.	New Bedford.	

7 September, 1887.

HENRY ROGERS HAYDEN	Hartford, Conn.	
JOHN HAIGH	Somerville	Life Member, 1887.

5 October, 1887.

LORING WILLIAM PUFFER, D.D.S.	Brockton.	
WILLIAM WILFRED CAMPBELL (Rev.)	Claremont, N.H.	6 November, 1889.
THOMAS RUTHERFORD TROWBRIDGE	New Haven, Conn.	
LINUS EVERETT PEARSON	Charlestown.	

7 December, 1887.

LEVI EDWIN DUDLEY	Boston	6 November, 1889.
HENRY WILLIAMS, A.B.	Boston.	
CHARLES THUILLIER MALLAPERT POWELL	Roxbury	Died 29 May, 1889.

4 January, 1888.

BABSON SAVILIAN LADD, A.B.	Boston.	

1 February, 1888.

FRANK WILLIAM ANDREWS	Boston.	
FREDERICK SMYTH, A.M.	Manchester, N.H.	
ELIJAH ADAMS MORSE	Canton.	
ISAAC WEARE HAMMOND, A.M.	Concord, N.H.	Died 28 September, 1890.
ROBERT INGLEE CARTER	Jamaica Plain	Fees commuted, 1889.
EZRA HOYT BYINGTON, A.M., D.D.	Worcester.	
HENRY WILLIAM MOULTON	Newburyport	1 July, 1891.

7 March, 1888.

NAME.	RESIDENCE.	MEMBERSHIP CEASED.
ALEXANDER HAMILTON LADD . .	Portsmouth, N. H.	1 July, 1891.
ALFRED ROGERS TURNER	Malden.	
WILLIAM HENRY COBB (Rev.). A.B.	Newton.	
ALFRED PORTER PUTNAM, A.B., D.D.	Concord . .	See 5 October, 1859. See Corresponding Roll, 7 December, 1864.

4 April, 1888.

WILLIAM PRENTISS PARKER . . .	Roxbury.	
WILLIAM LEONARD BENEDICT . .	Boston . .	Resigned 5 January, 1891.
WILLIAM LITTLE	Newbury.	

6 June, 1888.

EDWARD ISAIAH THOMAS . . .	Brookline .	Fees commuted, 1890. Died 26 December, 1890.
GUSTAVUS ARTHUR HILTON, LL.B.	Boston . . .	Fees commuted, 1892.
WALTER FREDERIC BROOKS . . .	Worcester.	
CHARLES AUGUSTUS GREENE, M.D.	Harrisburg, Pa.	
CHARLES THORNTON DAVIS, A.B. .	Boston.	
WINTHROP CHURCH WINSLOW, A.B.	Boston.	
JOHN ALEXANDER HAMILTON, A.B., D.D.	Boston.	

3 October, 1888.

LEMUEL LE BARON HOLMES, S.B. .	New Bedford.	
JAMES HENRY LEA	Fairhaven.	
GEORGE DAVID AYERS, A.B., LL.B.	Malden.	
THEODORE FRELINGHUYSEN DWIGHT	Quincy.	
FISKE WARREN, A.B.	Boston . . .	Fees commuted, 1891.
EDWARD KNOWLES BUTLER, Jr., A.B.	Boston . .	1 July, 1891.
FREDERICK BILLINGS, A.M., LL.D.	Woodstock,Vt.	Died 30 September, 1890.
CHARLES KNOWLES BOLTON, A.B. .	Cambridge.	
ARTHUR FREDERICK MEANS, LL.B.	Boston.	

7 November, 1888.

JOHN WILSON	Cambridge.	

5 December, 1888.

FRANCIS HENRY BROWN, A.M., M.D.	Boston . . .	See 4 February, 1874.

2 January, 1889.

JAMES BARRETT, A.M., LL.D. . .	Rutland, Vt. .	Fees commuted, 1889.
ENOCH STAFFORD JOHNSON . . .	Lynn . . .	Fees commuted, 1889.
ELLIOTT OTIS JOHNSON	Lynn.	

Name.	Residence.	Membership ceased.
Frank Mortimer Hawes, A.M.	Somerville.	
George H Norman [1]	Boston.	
Alfred Kingsley Glover (Rev.)	Cambridge	Resigned 24 March, 1891.

3 April, 1889.

Name.	Residence.	Membership ceased.
Samuel Merrill, A.B., LL.B.	Cambridge	Fees commuted, 1891.
George Wellman Wright	Duxbury.	
Dwight Eliot Bowers, A.B.	New Haven, Conn.	Fees commuted, 1889.
William James Wright	Duxbury.	
John Freeman Brown, A.B., LL.B.	Milton.	
Richard Walden Hale	Boston	Fees commuted, 1889.
Henry Augustus Root	Boston.	
Alden Perley White, A.B.	Danvers.	
Stephen Salisbury, A.M., LL.B.	Worcester	Fees commuted, 1889.
Thomas French Temple	Boston	1 July, 1891.
Frank Vernon Wright, A.B., S.B.	Salem	1 July, 1891.

1 May, 1889.

Name.	Residence.
Alexander Graham Bell, Ph.D., M.D.	Boston.
Stephen Henry Phillips, A.B., LL.B.	Salem.

5 June, 1889.

Name.	Residence.
Charles Henry Norris	Salem.

6 November, 1889.

Name.	Residence.	Membership ceased.
Eliot Dawes Stetson, A.B.	New Bedford.	
William Barnes	Marlborough.	
Julius Gay, Ph.B., A.M.	Farmington, Conn.	
Francis Minot Weld, A.M., M.D.	Jamacia Plain	Fees commuted, 1889.
Robert Thaxter Swan	Boston.	
Charles Sidney Ensign, LL.B.	Watertown	Fees commuted. 1889.
John Calvin Crane	Millbury.	
Lloyd Vernon Briggs	Hanover	Fees commuted, 1890.
Elisha Benjamin Andrews, A.M., D.D., LL.D.	Providence, R.I.	

[1] Mr Norman has no middle name, but uses "H" as a designation.

4 December, 1889.

NAME.	RESIDENCE.	MEMBERSHIP CEASED.
ORRIN PEER ALLEN	Palmer.	
WALTER KENDALL WATKINS . . .	Chelsea . .	Fees commuted, 1889.
THOMAS FOSDICK MILLETT . . .	Boston . . .	Resigned 8 June, 1891.
ARTHUR THEODORE CONNOLLY, D.B.	Boston.	
EDWARD NORRIS SULLIVAN . . .	Boston.	
JOHN CORDNER (Rev.), LL.D. . .	Boston . .	See Corresponding Roll, 3 August, 1859.
JAMES SEYMOUR GRINNELL, A.M. .	Greenfield .	See Corresponding Roll, 2 April, 1873.
GEORGE HERBERT PATTERSON (Rev.), A.M., LL.B.	Portsmouth, R. I.	See Corresponding Roll, 6 January, 1875.
WILLIAM APPLETON THOMAS . . .	Kingston.	

1 January, 1890.

ALMON DANFORTH HODGES, Jr., A.M.	Boston . . .	Fees commuted, 1890.

5 March, 1890.

HORACE LESLIE WHEELER, A.M., S.T.B.	Newton.	
ELIJAH BRIGHAM PHILLIPS . . .	Boston.	
NATHAN HAGAR DANIELS . . .	Boston . . .	See 6 January, 1869.
CHARLES SEDGWICK RACKEMANN .	Milton . . .	Fees commuted, 1890.

2 April, 1890.

WARREN BARTLETT ELLIS . . .	Boston.	
FRANCIS GREENLEAF PRATT, Jr. .	Boston . .	Fees commuted, 1890.
WILLIAM PITT BRECHIN, M.D. . .	Boston.	
GEORGE MARSHALL FELLOWS, A.B.	Hyde Park.	
FRANCIS VERGNIES BALCH, A.B., LL.B.	Boston.	
WILLIAM REUBEN RICHARDS, A.M., LL.B.	Boston . .	Fees commuted, 1890.
THOMAS FRANKLIN EDMANDS . .	Boston . .	Fees commuted, 1890.
THOMAS DOANE	Charlestown .	Fees commuted, 1890.

7 May, 1890.

Name.	Residence.	Membership ceased.
Frank Edson Shedd, S.B. . . .	Jaffrey, N. H.	Fees commuted, 1890.
Charles Alfred Johnson . . .	Salem.	
Arthur Fitch Benson	Salem.	

4 June, 1890.

John Graham Moseley	Boston.	
Andrew McFarland Davis, S.B. .	Cambridge.	

1 October, 1890.

John Eli Blakemore	Boston.	
John Hitchcock	Boston.	
Stephen Willard Phillips . .	Salem.	
Abbott Lawrence, A.M., LL.B. .	Boston . .	See 4 November, 1874. Fees commuted, 1891.
Roger Wolcott, A.B., LL.B. . .	Boston.	
Uriel Haskell Crocker, A.M., LL.B.	Boston.	
Edmund Hatch Bennett, A.M., LL.D.	Boston . .	See 2 February, 1870.
Henry Winchester Cunningham, A.B.	Boston . .	Fees commuted, 1891.
Alexander McKenzie, A.M., D.D.	Cambridge .	See 2 November, 1870.
David Rice Whitney, A.M. . .	Boston.	
Ira Joseph Patch.	Salem.	

5 November, 1890.

Charles Frank Mason, A.B. . .	Cambridge.	
Edward Francis Johnson, A.B., LL.B.	Woburn.	
Otis Norcross, A.B., LL.B. . .	Boston . .	Fees commuted, 1890.
Edward Wheelwright, A.M. . .	Boston . .	Fees commuted, 1890.
Julius Herbert Tuttle	Dedham.	
Samuel Swett Green, A.M. . .	Worcester .	Fees commuted, 1891.
William Cross Williamson, A.M., LL.B.	Boston.	
Eugene Bigelow Hagar, A.M., LL.B.	Boston . .	See 5 June, 1883. Fees commuted, 1891.

3 December, 1890.

NAME.	RESIDENCE.	MEMBERSHIP CEASED.
WILLIAM ALEXANDER MACLEOD, A.B., S.B., LL.B.	Dorchester.	
CHARLES LANGDON MITCHELL (Rev.), A.M.	Winchester.	
GRANVILLE STANLEY HALL, A.M., Ph.D., LL.D.	Worcester.	
HENRY GUSTAVUS DORR	Roxbury.	
MOSES WILLIAMS, A.B.	Brookline.	
EDWARD LIVINGSTON DAVIS, A.M.	Worcester .	Fees commuted, 1891.
GEORGE VASMER LEVERETT, A.M., LL.B.	Cambridge .	Fees commuted, 1891.
JEREMIAH EVARTS GREENE, A.B. .	Worcester.	
JAMES DE NORMANDIE (Rev.), A.M.	Roxbury.	
GEORGE WIGGLESWORTH, A.M., LL.B.	Boston.	
CHARLES AUGUSTUS CHASE, A.M. .	Worcester.	
FRANK BREWSTER, A.M., LL.B. .	Boston . .	Fees commuted, 1890.
ARCHIBALD MURRAY HOWE, A.M., LL.B.	Cambridge.	
FREDERIC WARD PUTNAM, A.M. .	Cambridge.	

7 January, 1891.

JAMES HOLDEN YOUNG, A.B., LL.B.	Boston.	
SAMUEL WELLS, A.B.	Boston.	
SHERMAN LELAND WHIPPLE, A.B., LL.B.	Brookline.	
FRANCIS BACON TROWBRIDGE, A.B., LL.B.	New Haven, Conn.	. Fees commuted, 1891.

4 February, 1891.

ANDREW FISKE, A.M., LL.B., Ph.D.	Boston . . .	Fees commuted, 1891.
EVERETT BOYNTON, A.M. .	Swampscott.	
HOWARD REDWOOD GUILD . .	Providence, R. I.	

4 March, 1891.

THOMAS WETMORE BISHOP (Rev.), A.M.	Boston.	
FREDERIC ENDICOTT	Canton.	
DARWIN ERASTUS WARE, A.M., LL.B.	Boston.	
ALBERT DAVIS BOSSON, A.M. . .	Chelsea.	
GEORGE OTIS SHATTUCK, A.B., LL.B.	Boston.	

1 April, 1891.

Name.	Residence.	Membership ceased.
William Jerdone Pettus, M. D.	Chelsea.	
Charles White Huntington (Rev.), A. B.	Lowell.	
William Gray Brooks, LL. B. . .	Boston.	
Frederick Dabney, A. B. . . .	Boston.	
Allen Danforth, A. M. . . .	Cambridge.	
Samuel Hooper Hooper . . .	Boston.	
Nathaniel Cushing Nash, A. B.	Boston.	
Frederic Tudor, Jr.	Boston.	
Solomon Lincoln, A. M., LL. B.	Boston.	
Walter Channing, M. D. . . .	Brookline.	
John Homans, 2d, A. B., M. D. .	Boston.	
John Low Rogers Trask, A. M., D. D.	Springfield.	

6 May, 1891.

John Elbridge Hudson, A. B., LL. B.	Boston.	
Edmund March Wheelwright, A. B.	Boston.	
Robert Tillinghast Babson, A. B., LL. B.	Gloucester.	
Charles Sherburne Penhallow, A. B.	Boston.	
John Chester Inches	Boston . . .	Fees commuted, 1891.
William Augustus Crombie . .	Burlington, Vt.	
George Henry Morse	Burlington, Vt.	
Richard Middlecott Saltonstall, A. B.	Newton.	
Waldo Lincoln, A. B.	Worcester.	
Francis Cabot Lowell, A. B. .	Boston.	

3 June, 1891.

Charles Frederic Crehore, M. D.	Newton.	
Alvah Crocker, A. B.	Fitchburg . .	Fees commuted, 1891.
Edward Elbridge Salisbury, A. M., LL. D.	New Haven, Conn.	
George Augustus Sawyer, A. B.	Cambridge.	
John Wilkins Carter	Newton.	
Edward Everett Hale, A. M., D. D.	Roxbury . .	See 5 August, 1846. Fees commuted, 1891.
Walbridge Abner Field, A. B., LL. D.	Boston.	

NAME.	RESIDENCE.	MEMBERSHIP CEASED.
AUGUSTUS GEORGE BULLOCK, A.M.	Worcester . .	Fees commuted, 1891.
THOMAS CHASE, A. M., Litt. D., LL. D.	Providence, R. I.	
WILLIAM HENRY PULSIFER . .	Newton.	

7 October, 1891.

HENRY PENNIMAN BLISS	Boston.	
SAMUEL CROCKER LAWRENCE, A.M.	Medford . .	Fees commuted, 1891.
JOHN CALVIN SPOFFORD . . .	Everett.	
GEORGE EDWARD POLLARD . .	Charlestown.	
HERBERT JOSEPH HARWOOD, A.B.	Littleton.	

4 November, 1891.

HORATIO ROGERS, A.B.	Providence, R. I.	
JOHN NOBLE, A. B., LL. B. . . .	Roxbury.	
JOSEPH HENRY ALLEN, A. M., D. D.	Cambridge.	
ISAAC NEWTON NUTTER	E. Bridgewater.	
HOWARD NICHOLSON BROWN (Rev.)	Brookline.	
CHARLES FREDERIC CHAMBERLAYNE, A. B., LL. B.	Bourne.	
WALTER ELA, A. B., M. D. . . .	Cambridge.	
JOHN ALBERT BUCKINGHAM (Rev.)	Newton.	
ARTHUR EASTMAN WHITNEY . .	Winchester .	Fees commuted, 1891.
THOMAS HOOPER, Jr.	Boston.	

2 December, 1891.

WILLIAM EUSTIS RUSSELL, A. B., LL. B., LL. D.	Cambridge .	Fees commuted, 1891.
WILLIAM GOODWIN RUSSELL, A. B., LL. B., LL. D.	Boston.	
JOHN LOWELL, A. M., LL. B., LL. D.	Newton.	
CHARLES FRANCIS ADAMS, A. B. .	Quincy .	. Fees commuted, 1891.
ALFRED MANSFIELD BROOKS . .	Gloucester.	
ELIJAH BRIGHAM STODDARD, A. M.	Worcester.	
FREDERICK FRANCIS WOODWARD .	Fitchburg.	
WILLIAM BABCOCK WEEDEN, A. M.	Providence, R. I.	
RICHARD ELA, A. B., LL. B. . .	Cambridge.	
FRANK PALMER GOULDING, A. B.	Worcester.	
REUBEN COLTON, A. B.	Worcester.	

List of Honorary Members.

20 February, 1845.

4 November, 1846.

NAME.	RESIDENCE.	MEMBERSHIP CEASED.
BENJAMIN SHURTLEFF, A.M., M.B., M.D.	Boston . . .	Died 12 April, 1847.
ROBERT GOULD SHAW	Boston .	Died 3 May, 1853.

6 January, 1847.

LEMUEL SHAW, A.M., LL.D. . .	Boston . . .	Died 30 March, 1861.
CHARLES LOWELL, A.M., D.D. . .	Boston . . .	Died 20 January, 1861.
RICHARD SULLIVAN, A.M. . . .	Boston . .	Died 11 December, 1861.
DUDLEY HALL	Medford. . .	Died 3 November, 1868.
AMOS LAWRENCE	Boston . .	Died 31 December, 1852.
JOSEPH SEWALL	Boston . .	Died 5 May, 1850.
JAMES BROWN THORNTON . . .	Saco, Me. . .	Life Member, 1871. Died 13 February, 1873.
SAMUEL HUBBARD, A.M., LL.D. .	Boston . . .	Died 24 December, 1847.
SAMUEL SUMNER WILDE, A.M., LL.D.	Boston . . .	Died 22 June, 1855.
ABEL CUSHING, A.B.	Boston . .	Elected Resident Member, 3 September, 1862.
SAMUEL HOAR, A.M., LL.D. . .	Concord . . .	Died 2 November, 1856.
NATHAN APPLETON, A.M., LL.D. . .	Boston . . .	Elected Resident Member, 6 April, 1853.
JONATHAN PHILLIPS, A.M. . . .	Boston . . .	Died 29 July, 1860.

3 February, 1847.

GEORGE NIXON BRIGGS, A.M., LL.D.	Boston . . .	Died 12 September, 1861.
WILLIAM HICKLING PRESCOTT, A.M., D.C.L., LL.D.	Boston . . .	Died 28 January, 1859.
RUFUS CHOATE, A.M., LL.D. . .	Boston . .	Died 13 July, 1859.
PELEG SPRAGUE, A.M., LL.D. .	Boston . .	Died 13 October, 1880.
GEORGE CHEYNE SHATTUCK, A.M., M.D., LL.D.	Boston . . .	Died 18 March, 1854.
DANIEL APPLETON WHITE, A.M., LL.D.	Salem . . .	Died 30 March, 1861.

3 March, 1847.

DANIEL WEBSTER, A.M., LL.D. .	Boston . . .	Died 24 October, 1852.
ALBERT GALLATIN,[1] LL.D. . . .	New York, N.Y.	Died 12 August, 1849.
WILLIAM CRANCH, A.M., LL.D. .	Washington, D.C.	Died 1 September, 1855.
CHARLES HENRY WARREN, A.M. .	Boston . . .	Died 29 June, 1874.

[1] Mr. Gallatin's original name was Abraham Alfonse Albert Gallatin.

NAME.	RESIDENCE.	MEMBERSHIP CEASED.
HENRY CLAY, LL. D.	Lexington, Ky.	Died 29 June, 1852.
BENJAMIN SILLIMAN, A. M., M. D., LL. D.	New Haven, Conn.	Died 24 November, 1864.
DANIEL PINCKNEY PARKER . . .	Boston . . .	See Resident Roll, 6 January, 1847. Died 31 August, 1850.

7 April, 1847.

ISAAC P DAVIS[1]	Boston . . .	Died 13 January, 1855.
JOHN DAVIS, A. M., LL. D. . . .	Worcester . .	Died 19 April, 1854.
WASHINGTON IRVING, A. M., D. C. L., LL. D.	Tarrytown, N. Y.	Died 28 November, 1859.
JAMES KENT, A. M., LL. D. . . .	New York, N. Y.	Died 12 December, 1847.
TIMOTHY PITKIN, A. M., LL. D. .	Utica, N. Y. .	Died 18 December, 1847.
THERON METCALF, A. M., LL. D. .	Boston . . .	Died 13 November, 1875.
LEWIS CASS, LL. D.	Detroit, Mich. .	Died 17 June, 1866.

5 May, 1847.

JAMES CUSHING MERRILL, A. M. .	Boston . . .	Died 4 October, 1853.

1 September, 1847.

LEVI WOODBURY, A. M., LL. D. .	Portsmouth, N. H.	Died 4 September, 1851.
DAVID HENSHAW	Leicester . .	Died 11 November, 1852.

1 March, 1848.

CHARLES AUGUSTUS DEWEY, A. M., LL. D.	Northampton .	Died 22 August, 1866.
MAHLON DICKERSON, A. M. .	Suckasunny, N. J.	Died 5 October, 1853.

6 February, 1850.

SAMUEL BRECK	Philadelphia, Pa.	Died 1 September, 1862.
WILLIAM EDWARDS MAYHEW . .	Baltimore, Md.	Died 11 April, 1860.
THOMAS SERGEANT, A. M. . . .	Philadelphia, Pa.	Died 8 May, 1860.

5 May, 1852.

GEORGE PEABODY, D. C. L., LL. D.	London, Eng. .	Died 4 November, 1869.

2 March, 1853.

NOAH MARTIN, M. D.	Dover, N. H. .	Died 28 May, 1863.

[1] Mr. Davis had no middle name, but used "P" as a designation.

1 February, 1854.

NAME.	RESIDENCE.	MEMBERSHIP CEASED.
RUSSELL STURGIS, A. M.	London, Eng. .	Died 2 November, 1887.

7 June, 1854.

MILLARD FILLMORE, LL. D. . . . Buffalo, N.Y. . See Corresponding Roll, 18 June, 1845. Died 8 March, 1874.

5 July, 1854.

GUSTAVUS SWAN . . . . . . Columbus, Ohio Died 7 February, 1860.

1 November, 1854.

JOHN WHEELER, A. M., D. D. . . Burlington, Vt. Died 16 April, 1862.

3 January, 1855.

JOHN COLLINS WARREN, A. M., M. D. Boston . . . Died 4 May, 1856.

4 April, 1855.

WILLIAM ALLEN, A.M., D.D. . . Northampton . See Corresponding Roll, 4 February, 1846. Died 16 July, 1868.

3 October, 1855.

JOSEPH BARLOW FELT (Rev.), A.M., LL. D. Boston . . . See Corresponding Roll, 20 March, 1845; and Resident Roll, June 2, 1847. Died 8 September. 1869.

3 August, 1859.

JAMES WALKER, A. M., D. D., LL. D. Cambridge Died 24 December, 1874.
TIMOTHY FARRAR, A. M., LL. D. . Dorchester See Resident Roll, 6 February, 1850. Died 27 October, 1874.

7 December, 1859.

JOHN TYLER, A. B., LL. D. . . . Charles City, Va. Died 17 January, 1862.

4 January, 1860.

SAMUEL GARDNER DRAKE, A. M. . Boston . . . See Resident Roll, 17 December, 1844. Died 14 June, 1875.

11 July, 1860.

CORNELIUS CONWAY FELTON, A. M., Cambridge . . Died 26 February, 1862. LL. D.

2 January, 1861.

NAME.	RESIDENCE.	MEMBERSHIP CEASED.
JOSEPH RICHARDSON (Rev.), A. M.	Hingham . .	See Resident Roll, 6 May, 1857. Died 25 September, 1871.

1 May, 1861.

Sir FREDERICK MADDEN, F.S.A. . London, Eng. . Died 8 March, 1873.

WILLIAM WILLIS, A. M., LL. D. . Portland, Me. . See Corresponding Roll, 20 March, 1845. Died 17 February, 1870.

5 June, 1861.

LOUIS ADOLPHE THIERS . . . Paris, France . Died 3 September, 1877.

6 November, 1861.

GEORGE RAPALL NOYES, A.M., D. D. Cambridge . . Died 3 June, 1868.

6 August, 1862.

EZEKIEL WHITMAN, A.B., LL. D. . Bridgewater . Died 1 August, 1866.

5 November, 1862.

THOMAS HILL, A. M., D. D., LL. D. Cambridge . . Died 21 November, 1891.

3 December, 1862.

Sir JOHN BERNARD BURKE, C. B., Dublin, Ireland See Corresponding Roll,
LL. D., M. R. I. A.   5 November, 1851.

7 January, 1863.

Sir THOMAS PHILLIPPS, Bart., M. A., Broadway . . Died 6 February, 1872.
F. R. S.   Worcester, Eng.

7 October, 1863.

EDWIN AUGUSTINE DALRYMPLE, Baltimore, Md. See Corresponding Roll,
D. D.   7 December, 1859. Died 30 October, 1881.

3 February, 1864.

PHILIP HENRY STANHOPE, Earl London, Eng. . Died 24 December, 1875.
Stanhope, M. A., D. C. L., LL. D.,
F. R. S., F. S. A.

2 March, 1864.

FRANÇOIS PIERRE GUILLAUME Paris, France . Died 13 September, 1874.
GUIZOT, LL. D., F. S. A.

2 August, 1865.

REUBEN HYDE WALWORTH, LL. D.   Saratoga Springs, See Corresponding Roll,
                               N. Y.   4 November, 1857.
                                               Died 21 November, 1867.

5 September, 1866.

HORACE BINNEY, A. M., LL. D. . .   Philadelphia, Pa. Died 12 August, 1875.

3 February, 1869.

ULYSSES SIMPSON GRANT,[1] U. S. A.,   Washington, D.C. Died 23 July, 1885.
   LL. D.

6 November, 1872.

NATHAN CLIFFORD, LL. D. . . .   Washington, D.C. Died 25 July, 1881.

2 June, 1875.

JOSEPH SMITH, U. S. N.   . . . .   Washington, D.C. Died 17 January, 1877.

5 April, 1876.

JOHN JOHNSTON, A. M., LL. D. . .   Middletown,   Died 3 December, 1879.
                                   Conn.

3 October, 1877.

RUTHERFORD BIRCHARD HAYES,   Washington, D.C.
   A. M., LL. B., LL. D.

3 December, 1879.

JOHN GEORGE EDWARD HENRY   Ottawa, Can.
   DOUGLAS SUTHERLAND CAMP-
   BELL, Marquis of Lorne, K. T.,
   G. C. M. G., B. A., D. Litt., LL. D.

2 January, 1884.

CHESTER ALAN ARTHUR, A. M.,   Washington, D.C. Died 18 November, 1886.
   LL. D.

6 February, 1884.

WILLIAM EWART GLADSTONE, M. A.,   Hawarden, Flint,
   D. C. L., LL. D., F. R. S.   Wales.

5 May, 1886.

MORRISON REMICK WAITE, A. M.,   Washington, D.C. Died 23 March, 1888.
   LL. D.

[1] President Grant's original name was Hiram Ulysses Grant.

1 October, 1890.[1]

NAME.	RESIDENCE.	MEMBERSHIP CEASED.
BENSON JOHN LOSSING, A.M., LL.D.	Dover Plains, N. Y.	See Corresponding Roll, 7 May, 1851. Died 3 June, 1891.
GEORGE HENRY MOORE, A.M., LL.D.	New York, N.Y.	See Corresponding Roll, 4 April, 1855. Died 5 May, 1892.
JOHN GILMARY SHEA, LL. D.	Elizabeth, N.J.	See Corresponding Roll, 2 February, 1859. Died 22 February, 1892.
DAVID MASSON, M.A., LL. D. . .	Edinburgh, Scot.	See Corresponding Roll, 3 August, 1859.
JAMES MACPHERSON LE MOINE, F. R. S. C.	Quebec, Can. .	See Corresponding Roll, 9 October, 1875.
GEORGE WILLIAM CURTIS, A.M., L. H. D., LL. D.	New Brighton, N. Y.	See Corresponding Roll, 7 February, 1883.
NATHANIEL HOLMES MORISON, A.M., LL. D.	Baltimore, Md.	See Corresponding Roll, 2 April, 1884. Died 14 November, 1890.
Sir JOHN CAMPBELL ALLEN, LL. D.	Fredericton, N. B.	See Corresponding Roll, 4 June, 1884.
EDWARD AUGUSTUS FREEMAN, M.A., D. C. L., LL. D.	Wells, Somerset, Eng.	See Corresponding Roll, 7 January, 1885. Died 16 March, 1892.
CHARLES KENDALL ADAMS, A.M., LL. D.	Ann Arbor, Mich.	See Corresponding Roll, 4 February, 1885.
Sir THEODORE MARTIN, K.C.B., LL.D.	Bath, Somerset, Eng.	See Corresponding Roll, 1 April, 1885.
JAMES ANTHONY FROUDE, M. A. .	London, Eng.	See Corresponding Roll, 1 December, 1886.

5 November, 1890.

JAMES BRYCE, B. A., B. C. L., D.C. L. London, Eng.

3 December, 1890.

WILLIAM EDWARD HARTPOLE London, Eng.
LECKY, M. A., D. C. L., LL. D.

[1] In the autumn of 1890 the Honorary Roll bore but six names, none having been added to it for more than four years, while only three names had been added during the preceding decade. The number of Honorary Members being out of all proportion to the number of Corresponding and Resident Members, the Society, at its Stated Meeting in October, transferred from the Corresponding Roll to the Honorary Roll the names of twelve gentlemen who were among those of its Fellows who had distinguished themselves in the department of History rather than in that of Genealogy.

1 April, 1891.

NAME.	RESIDENCE.	MEMBERSHIP CEASED.

WILLIAM WETMORE STORY, A.M.,   Rome, Italy.
   LL. B., D. C. L.

7 October, 1891.

ANDREW DICKSON WHITE, A. M.,   Ithaca, N. Y.
   L. H. D., LL. D.

2 December, 1891.

MELVILLE WESTON FULLER, A.M.,   Washington,
   LL.D.   D. C.

List of Corresponding Members.

21 January, 1845.

NAME.	RESIDENCE.	MEMBERSHIP CEASED.
SAMUEL FOSTER HAVEN, A.M., LL. D.	Worcester . .	Died 5 September, 1881.
WILLIAM PLUMER, Jr., A.M.	Epping, N. H. .	Died 18 September, 1854.
NATHANIEL GOOKIN UPHAM, A.M., LL. D.	Concord, N. H.	Died 11 December, 1869.
THOMAS ROBBINS, A.M., D. D. .	Hartford, Conn.	Died 13 September, 1856.

6 February, 1845.

SAMUEL HOLDEN PARSONS, A. M.	Hartford, Conn.	Life Member, 1865. Died 23 February, 1871.
JOHN DAGGETT, A.M.	Attleborough .	Died 13 December, 1885.
HENRY GOOKIN STORER (Rev.), A.M.	Scarborough, Me.	Died 19 September, 1888.
JOHN PRENTISS, A.M. . . .	Keene, N. H. .	Died 6 June, 1873.

7 March, 1845.

MARK ANTONY LOWER, M.A., F.S.A.	Lewes, Sussex, Eng.	Died 22 March, 1876.

20 March, 1845.

JAMES ATHEARN JONES . . .	Tisbury . . .	Died 7 July, 1854.
JOSEPH BARLOW FELT (Rev.), A.M., LL.D.	Boston . . .	Elected Resident Member, 2 June, 1847. See Honorary Roll, 5 October, 1855.
WILLIAM WILLIS, A.M., LL.D.	Portland, Me. .	Elected Honorary Member, 1 May, 1861.
HENRY BOND, A.M., M.D. . .	Philadelphia. Pa.	Died 4 May, 1859.
JOSIAH ADAMS, A.M.	Framingham .	Died 8 February, 1854.

1 April, 1845.

ALBERT GORTON GREENE. A.B.	Providence, R. I.	Died 3 January, 1868.
USHER PARSONS, A.M., M.D. .	Providence, R. I.	Elected Resident Member, 3 August, 1864.

15 April, 1845.

NAME.	RESIDENCE.	MEMBERSHIP CEASED.
ELISHA THAYER	Dedham . . .	Died 9 June, 1860.
HENRY OLCOTT SHELDON (Rev.)	Berea, Ohio . .	Died 21 December, 1882.
CHARLES WILLIAM BRADLEY (Rev.), A. M., LL. D.	Hartford, Conn.	Died 8 March, 1865.

7 May, 1845.

NAHUM MITCHELL, A. M. . . .	Plymouth . .	See Resident Roll, 6 February, 1845. Died 1 August, 1853.

4 June, 1845.

GURDON TRUMBULL	Stonington, Conn.	Died 8 October, 1875.
SAMUEL SEWALL (Rev.), A.M. .	Burlington . .	Died 18 February, 1868.
SAMUEL JOHN CARR. M.D. . .	Baltimore, Md.	Died 24 October, 1847.
SAMUEL WEBBER, A. M., M. D. .	Charlestown, N.H.	Died 5 December, 1880.
MELLEN CHAMBERLAIN, A. B., LL. B., LL. D.	Boston.	
ELLIS AMES, A.B.	Canton . . .	Died 30 October, 1884.

18 June, 1845.

JOSHUA COFFIN, A. M.	Newbury . . .	Died 24 June, 1864.
BENJAMIN FRANKLIN THOMPSON	Hempstead, N. Y.	Died 22 March, 1849.
LEONARD BACON, A.M., D.D., LL. D.	New Haven, Conn.	Died 24 December, 1881.
SAMUEL WHITCOMB, Jr. . . .	Springfield, Vt.	Died 5 March, 1879.
MILLARD FILLMORE, LL. D. . .	Buffalo, N. Y. .	Elected Honorary Member, 7 June, 1854.
CHARLES KILBOURNE WILLIAMS, A. M., LL. D.	Rutland, Vt. .	Died 9 March, 1853.
JAMES WHITCOMB	Indianapolis, Ind.	Died 6 October, 1852.

1 July, 1845.

ALBERT SMITH WHITE, A.M. .	Lafayette, Ind..	Died 4 September, 1864.
WILLIAM TYLER (Rev.), A.M. .	Amherst . . .	Died 27 September, 1875.
LEWIS BRADFORD	Plympton . .	Died 10 August, 1851.

6 August, 1845.

SAMUEL ADAMS TURNER . . .	Scituate . . .	Died 7 June, 1890.
JOHN FROST, A. M., LL. D. . .	Philadelphia, Pa.	Died 28 December, 1859.
JOSEPH DOW, A.M.	Hampton, N. H.	Died 16 December, 1889.
ELEAZER WILLIAMS (Rev.) . .	Green Bay, Wis.	Died 28 August, 1858.

Name.	Residence.	Membership ceased.
Samuel Ames, A. M., LL. D.	Providence, R. I.	Died 20 December, 1865.
Amos Atwell Tillinghast . .	Pawtucket, R. I.	Died 19 March, 1859.
Oliver Alden Taylor (Rev.), A. M.	Manchester . .	Died 18 December, 1851.
William Durkee Williamson, A. M.	Bangor, Me. .	Died 27 May, 1846.
John Howland, A. M.	Providence, R. I.	Died 5 November, 1854.

3 September, 1845.

James Ward	Hartford, Conn.	Died 25 October, 1856.
Seth Chandler (Rev.) . . .	Shirley . . .	Died 4 October, 1889.
John Appleton, A. M., LL. D. .	Bangor, Me. .	Died 7 February, 1891.
Stephen Fales, A. M.	Cincinnati, Ohio	Died 3 September, 1854.

7 October, 1845.

Lot Edward Brewster . . .	Cincinnati, Ohio	Died 21 June, 1849.
George Sparhawk	Kittery, Me. .	Died 21 November, 1857.
George Folsom, A. M., LL. D. .	New York, N. Y.	Died 27 March, 1869.

4 November, 1845.

Nathaniel Chauncey, A. M. .	Philadelphia, Pa.	Life Member, 1862. Died 9 February, 1865.

6 January, 1846.

Jacob Bailey Moore	Washington, D.C.	Died 1 September, 1853.
Oliver Bliss Morris, A. M. .	Springfield . .	Died 9 April, 1871.
Andrew Randall	Cincinnati, Ohio	Died 26 July, 1856.
Stephen West Williams, A. M., M. D.	Deerfield . .	Died 9 July, 1855.

4 February, 1846.

Ebenezer Alden, A. M., M. D. .	Randolph . .	Life Member, 1864. Died 26 January, 1881.
William Allen, A. M., D D. .	Northampton .	Elected Honorary Member, 4 April, 1855.
Horace Day, A. M.	New Haven, Conn.	
Caleb Butler, A. M.	Groton . . .	Died 7 October, 1854.
Ralph Dunning Smith,[1] A. B .	Guilford, Conn.	Died 11 September, 1874.
Charles Jeremy Hoadly, A. M., LL. D.	Hartford, Conn.	
Jonathan French, A. M., D. D. .	North Hampton, N. H.	Died 13 December, 1856.

[1] Mr. Smith sometimes spelled his name " Smyth."

7 April, 1846.

NAME.	RESIDENCE.	MEMBERSHIP CEASED.
WILLIAM READ STAPLES, A.M., LL.D.	Providence, R.I.	Died 19 October, 1868.
ELIAL TODD FOOTE, M.D. . .	New Haven, Conn.	Died 17 November, 1877.
NATHANIEL GOODWIN	Hartford, Conn.	Died 29 May, 1855.
WILLIAM COGSWELL, A.M., D.D.	Gilmanton, N.H.	Died 18 April, 1850.
WILKINS UPDIKE, A.M. . . .	Kingston, R.I.	Died 14 January, 1867.
JOHN ANDREWS HOWLAND . .	Providence, R.I.	Died 24 October, 1889.
EMORY WASHBURN, A.M., LL.D.	Worcester . .	Died 18 March, 1877.
ELISHA REYNOLDS POTTER, A.B.	Kingston, R.I.	Died 10 April, 1882.
EDWIN HUBBARD	Meriden, Conn.	
HENRY WHEATLAND, A.M., M.D.	Salem.	

6 May, 1846.

WILLIAM ELY (Rev.), A.B. . .	Northampton .	Died 2 November, 1850.
SAMUEL PRESCOTT HILDRETH, M.D.	Marietta, Ohio .	Died 24 July, 1863.
JAMES DELAP FARNSWORTH (Rev.), A.M.	Boxborough . .	Died 12 November, 1854.
GEORGE ARNOLD BRAYTON, A.M., LL.D.	Warwick, R.I. .	Died 21 April, 1880.
DANIEL LANCASTER (Rev.), A.M.	Gilmanton, N.H.	Died 28 May, 1880.

3 June, 1846.

THOMAS EDWIN WHITNEY, A.M.	Shirley . . .	Died 25 October, 1876.
ABNER MORSE (Rev.), A.M. . .	South Bend, Ind.	Elected Resident Member, 5 September, 1860.

7 October, 1846.

JOHN JAMES BABSON	Gloucester . .	Died 13 April, 1886.
GUY MANNERING FESSENDEN .	Warren, R.I. .	Died 1 November, 1871.
LUCIUS MANLIUS BOLTWOOD, A.B.	Amherst.	

4 November, 1846.

ISRAEL WARBURTON PUTNAM, A.M., D.D.	Middleborough .	Died 3 May, 1868.
FREEMAN HUNT, A.M. . . .	New York, N.Y.	Died 2 March, 1858.

2 December, 1846.

THOMAS BELLOWS WYMAN, Jr. .	Charlestown .	Elected Resident Member, 10 January, 1850.

6 January, 1847.

Name.	Residence.	Membership ceased.
Noah Amherst Phelps . . .	Middletown,Conn.	Died 26 August, 1872.
Daniel Drake, M.D.	Cincinnati, Ohio	Died 5 November, 1852.
John Bathurst Deane (Rev.), M.A., F.S.A.	London, Eng. .	Died 12 July, 1887.
Jacob Wendell	Portsmouth, N.H.	Died 27 August, 1865.
Charles Turell	New York, N.Y.	Died 8 June, 1863.

3 February, 1847.

Caleb Cushing, A.M., LL.D.	Newburyport .	Died 2 January, 1879.
William Smith Porter . . .	Farmington,Conn.	Died 11 June, 1866.
Jonathan Marsh	Quincy . . .	Died 10 December, 1861.
Convers Francis, A.M., D.D. .	Cambridge . .	Died 7 April, 1863.
Charles Wentworth Upham (Rev.), A.M.	Salem	Died 15 June, 1875.

3 March, 1847.

James Davie Butler, A.M., LL.D.	Norwich, Vt.	
Nathaniel Bouton, A.M., D.D.	Concord, N.H. .	Died 6 June, 1878.
Elias Nason (Rev.), A.M. . .	Newburyport .	Elected Resident Member, 5 January, 1848.
William Chauncey, A.M. . .	New York, N.Y.	Died 20 June, 1870.
Salma Hale, A.M.	Keene, N.H. .	Died 19 November, 1866.
James Luce Kingsley, A.M., LL.D.	New Haven, Conn.	Died 31 August, 1852.
Joel Harvey Linsley, A.B., D.D.	Marietta, Ohio .	Died 22 March, 1868.
Job Roberts Tyson	Philadelphia, Pa.	Died 27 June, 1858.
William Buell Sprague, A.M., D.D., LL.D.	Albany, N.Y. .	Died 7 May, 1876.
Romeo Elton, A.M., D.D. . .	Exeter, Devon, Eng.	Died 5 February, 1870.

7 April, 1847.

Matthew Adams Stickney . .	Salem.	
Charles Frederick Sedgwick, A.M.	Sharon, Conn. .	Died 9 March, 1882.
Henry Barnard, A.M., L.H.D , LL.D.	Providence, R.I.	
Henry Alexander Scammell Dearborn, A.M.	Roxbury . . .	Died 29 July, 1851.
Royal Ralph Hinman, A.M. .	Hartford, Conn.	Died 16 October, 1868.
Thomas Day, A.M., LL.D. . .	Hartford, Conn.	Died 1 March, 1855.
William Baylies, A.M., LL.D.	West Bridgewater	Died 27 September, 1865.

5 May, 1847.

NAME.	RESIDENCE.	MEMBERSHIP CEASED.
BENJAMIN SILLIMAN, Jr., A.M., M.D., LL.D.	New Haven, Conn.	Died 14 January, 1885.
BENJAMIN DRAKE, M.D. . .	New York, N.Y.	Died 11 January, 1871.
JOB DURFEE, A.M., LL.D. . .	Tiverton, R.I. .	Died 26 July, 1847.
JOSEPH COURTEN HORNBLOWER, A.M., LL.D.	Newark, N.J. .	Died 11 June, 1864.
NICHOLAS MURRAY, A.M., D.D.	Elizabethtown, N.J.	Died 4 February, 1861.
GEORGE THOMAS DAVIS, LL.B.	Greenfield . .	Died 17 June, 1877.
WILLIAM PARSONS	Boston . . .	Elected Resident Member, 2 June, 1847.
GEORGE LUNT, A.B. . .	Newburyport .	Elected Resident Member, 4 April, 1855.
ANSEL PHELPS, Jr.	Springfield . .	Died 2 June, 1860.
JACOB HERSEY LOUD . . .	Plymouth . .	Died 2 February, 1880.
ALVAN LAMSON, A.M., D.D. .	Dedham . . .	Died 18 July, 1864.
HANNIBAL HAMLIN, LL.D. . .	Hampden, Me.	Died 4 July, 1891.
SAMUEL DANA BELL, A.B., LL.D.	Manchester, N.H.	Elected Resident Member, 4 May, 1858. Life Member, 1863. Died 31 July, 1868.
HENRY WYLES CUSHMAN . . .	Bernardston .	Elected Resident Member, 3 November, 1858.
SAMUEL BRAZER BABCOCK, A.M., D.D.	Dedham . .	Died 25 October, 1873.
LUTHER WAIT	Ipswich . . .	Died 20 October, 1847.
JOHN MASON PECK, A.M., D.D.	Rock Spring, Ill.	Died 14 March, 1858.
PAYNE KENYON KILBOURNE . .	Litchfield, Conn.	Died 19 July, 1859.
WILLIAM COTHREN, A.M. . .	Woodbury, Conn.	
AMOS BUGBEE CARPENTER . .	Waterford, Vt.	
GEORGE EDWARD DAY, A.M., D.D.	Marlborough .	30 November, 1869.
JOHN McLEAN, LL.D.	Cincinnati, Ohio	Died 4 April, 1861.
SAMUEL WRIGHT PHELPS . . .	Cincinnati, Ohio	Died 11 September, 1879.
NICHOLAS DEAN	New York, N.Y.	Died 21 December, 1855.

2 June, 1847.

GEORGE GIBBS, LL.B.	New York, N.Y.	Died 9 April, 1873.
CHARLES MOSES ENDICOTT . .	Salem	Died 15 December, 1863.
WILLIAM BARRY (Rev.), A.M. .	Framingham .	Died 17 January, 1885.

7 July, 1847.

AMOS OTIS	Yarmouth . .	Elected Resident Member, 7 March, 1855.

4 August, 1847.

LILLEY EATON	South Reading.	Elected Resident Member, 2 March, 1870.
DAVID DUDLEY FIELD, A.M., D.D.	Haddam, Conn.	Died 15 April, 1867.
CHAUNCEY COLTON, A.M., D.D.	Cincinnati, Ohio	Died 15 April, 1876.
EPHRAIM ABBOT (Rev.), A.M. .	Westford . .	Died 21 July, 1870.
HORATIO ALGER (Rev.), A.M. .	Marlborough .	Died 6 November, 1881.

1 September, 1847.

PETER FOLGER EWER	Nantucket . .	Died 7 January, 1855.
JOHN STEVENS ABBOTT, A.M. .	Norridgewock, Me.	Died 12 June, 1881.
FREDERICK HOBBS, A.M. . . .	Bangor, Me. .	Died 10 October, 1854.
WILLIAM PRESCOTT, M.D. . .	Concord, N.H.	Died 18 October, 1875.
LEVI WASHBURN LEONARD, A.M., D.D.	Dublin, N.H. .	Died 12 December, 1864.
MERRITT CALDWELL, A.M. . .	Carlisle, Pa. .	Died 6 June, 1848.
WILLIAM GAMMELL, A.M., LL.D.	Providence, R.I.	Elected Resident Member, 6 April, 1870.
CALVIN DURFEE, A.M., D.D. .	Dedham . . .	Died 21 November, 1879.
LINUS PIERPONT BROCKETT, A.M., M.D.	Hartford, Conn.	
JAMES ROYAL CUSHING (Rev.) .	Wells, Me. . .	Died 11 June, 1881.
AUGUSTUS DODGE ROGERS . .	Salem.	
EZEKIEL BACON, A.B.	Utica, N.Y.	Died 18 October, 1870.
STALHAM WILLIAMS	Utica, N.Y. .	Died 8 April, 1873.
FRANCIS VINTON, D.D., LL.D. .	Brooklyn, N.Y.	Died 29 September, 1872.
TRYON EDWARDS, A.M., D.D. .	New London, Conn.	

7 October, 1847.

OTIS WILBOR	Little Compton, R.I.	Died 15 January, 1856.
JOHN ORR (Rev.), A.M. . . .	Alfred, Me. . .	Died 25 January, 1869.
THEODORE CUSHING	Greece, N.Y. .	Died 13 January, 1850.

3 November, 1847.

ALFRED LOUIS BAURY, A.M., D.D.	Newton . . .	Died 26 December, 1865.
BENJAMIN LINCOLN SWAN (Rev.), A.M.	Litchfield, Conn.	

1 December, 1847.

JONATHAN GREENLEAF, A.M., D.D.	Brooklyn, N.Y.	Died 24 April, 1865.
MARK DOOLITTLE, A.M. . . .	Belchertown .	Died 7 November, 1855.

5 January, 1848.

NAME.	RESIDENCE.	MEMBERSHIP CEASED.
ZEDEKIAH SMITH BARSTOW, A.M., D.D.	Keene, N.H.	Died 1 March, 1873.
ISAAC MCCONIHE, A.M., LL.D.	Troy, N.Y.	Died 1 November, 1867.
JOSEPH HUNTER (Rev.), F.S.A.	London, Eng.	Died 9 May, 1861.
HENRY CRUSE MURPHY, A.B., LL.D.	Brooklyn, N.Y.	Died 1 December, 1882.
WILLIAM LEVERETT DICKINSON, A.M.	Jersey City, N.J.	Died 3 November, 1883.
EDWIN HALL, A.B., D.D.	Norwalk, Conn.	Died 8 September, 1877.
SAMUEL HOLDEN PARSONS HALL	Binghamton, N.Y.	Died 5 March, 1877.
SAMUEL CHURCH, A.B., LL.D.	Litchfield, Conn.	Died 13 September, 1854.

2 February, 1848.

CHARLES WARNER CADY	Indianapolis, Ind.	Died 19 November, 1855.

1 March, 1848.

SAMUEL WHITE THAYER, A.M., M.D., LL.D.	Northfield, Vt.	Died 14 November, 1882.
PHINEAS WASHINGTON LELAND, M.D.	Fall River	Died 22 January, 1870.
FREDERIC SALMON PEASE	Albany, N.Y.	Died 22 March, 1867.
GEORGE GAINES BREWSTER, M.D., D.D.S.	Portsmouth, N.H.	Died 7 July, 1872.

5 April, 1848.

THOMAS PRESTON GENTLEE	Manchester	Died 22 December, 1875.

4 October, 1848.

RICHARD MANNING CHIPMAN (Rev.), A.B.	Guilford, Conn.	

13 December, 1848.

WILLIAM IVES BUDINGTON, A.M., D.D.	Charlestown	See Resident Roll, 4 February, 1846. Died 29 November, 1879.

11 July, 1849.

LEONARD MOODY PARKER, A.M.	Shirley	Died 25 August, 1854.
JOSHUA GREEN, A.M., M.D.	Groton	Died 5 June, 1875.

6 February, 1850.

NAME.	RESIDENCE.	MEMBERSHIP CEASED.
SAMUEL WOLCOTT, A. M., D. D. .	Belchertown .	Died 24 February, 1886.

6 March, 1850.

WILLIAM SHAW RUSSELL . . . Plymouth   Died 22 February, 1863.

3 April, 1850.

SAMUEL HAZARD . . . . . . Philadelphia, Pa. Died 22 May, 1870.
EDWARD ARMSTRONG . . . . Philadelphia, Pa. Died 25 February, 1875.

5 June, 1850.

WILLIAM DOWNING BRUCE. F. S. A. London, Eng. . Died 13 October, 1875.
STEPHEN DODD (Rev.), A. M. . East Haven,   Died 5 February, 1856.
        Conn.

3 July, 1850.

AMZI BENEDICT DAVENPORT . Brooklyn, N. Y.

18 December, 1850.

WILLIAM CUSHING BINNEY, A. B., Amesbury . . Died 2 June, 1882.
    LL. B.
MORTIMER BLAKE, A. M.. D. D. Mansfield . . Died 22 December. 1884.
JOHN WENTWORTH, A. M., LL. D. Chicago, Ill. . Life Member, 1865.
            Died 16 October, 1888.

5 February, 1851.

CHANDLER EASTMAN POTTER. A.B. Manchester, N.H. Died 3 August, 1868.
BALLARD SMITH,[1] A. B. . . . Louisville, Ky. . Died 3 October, 1866.
NATHAN SARGENT . . . . . Washington, D.C. Died 2 February, 1875.
EDWARD KIDDER . . . . Wilmington, N. C. Life Member, 1871.
            Died 25 February, 1885.

7 May, 1851.

BENSON JOHN LOSSING, A. M., New York, N. Y. Elected Honorary Mem-
    LL. D.   ber, 1 October, 1890.

4 June, 1851.

SEBASTIAN FERRIS STREETER, Baltimore, Md. . Died 23 August, 1864.
    A. M.

2 July, 1851.

WILLIAM COLEMAN FOLGER . . Nantucket . . Died 10 November, 1891.

---

[1] Judge Smith's original name was William Ballard Smith.

13

6 August, 1851.

Name.	Residence.	Membership ceased.
Thomas Rutherford Trow-bridge	New Haven, Conn.	Died 26 May, 1887.

3 September, 1851.

Samuel Fulton Clarke (Rev.) Athol . . . . Died 27 March, 1861.

5 November, 1851.

Charles Henry Davis, U.S.N., A.M., LL.D.   Cambridge . .   Died 18 February, 1877.

Sir John Bernard Burke, C.B., LL.D., M.R.I.A.   London, Eng. .   Elected Honorary Member, 3 December, 1862.

7 January, 1852.

Horatio Gates Jones, Jr., A.M., D.C.L.   Philadelphia, Pa.

George Wadleigh . . . . .   Dover, N.H. .   Died 12 August, 1884.

4 February, 1852.

Alfred Hawkins . . . . .   Quebec, Can. .   Died 30 June, 1854.

3 March, 1852.

James Crosby . . . . . .   London, Eng. .   Died 12 July, 1867.

Samuel Tymms, F.S.A. . . .   Bury St.Edmunds, Suffolk, Eng.   Died 29 April, 1871.

5 May, 1852.

Oliver Mayhew Whipple . .   Lowell . . .   Elected Resident Member, 2 March, 1870.

Asa Warren Brown . . . .   Cincinnati, Ohio.

Nathaniel Sawyer, A.M. . .   Cincinnati, Ohio   Died 3 October, 1853.

3 June, 1852.

Samuel Bickerton Harman, D.C.L.   Toronto, Can.

4 August, 1852.

Elijah Hayward . . . . .   Columbus, Ohio   Died 22 September, 1864.

2 February, 1853.

Ashbel Woodward, M.D. . .   Franklin, Conn.   Died 20 December, 1885.

NAME.	RESIDENCE.	MEMBERSHIP CEASED.
WILLIAM GRIGSON (Rev.), M.A.	Whinburgh, Norfolk, Eng.	Died 6 October, 1879.
SHUBAEL BARTLETT (Rev.), A.M.	East Windsor, Conn.	Died 6 June, 1854.

6 April, 1853.

PHILO MALLORY TROWBRIDGE .	Woodbury, Conn.	Died 11 January, 1874.

5 October, 1853.

HENRY HARROD, F.S.A. . . .	Norwich, Norfolk, Eng.	Died 24 January, 1871.

1 February, 1854.

HENRY WHITE, A.M.	New Haven, Conn.	Died 7 October, 1880.
LYMAN COPELAND DRAPER, A.M., LL.D.	Madison, Wis. .	Died 26 August, 1891.

5 April, 1854.

JONATHAN PEARSON, A.M. . .	Schenectady, N.Y.	Died 20 June, 1887.

3 May, 1854.

EDMUND BAILEY O'CALLAGHAN, M.D., LL.D.	Albany, N.Y. .	Died 29 May, 1880.
CAMILLUS KIDDER	Baltimore, Md. .	September, 1866.

2 August, 1854.

JOSHUA VICTOR HOPKINS CLARK	Manlius, N.Y. .	Died 18 June, 1869.

6 September, 1854.

ROBERT ADAMS	Newbury. . .	Died 2 August 1855.

4 October, 1854.

ELIAS WARNER LEAVENWORTH, A.M., LL.D.	Albany, N.Y. .	Died 25 November, 1887.
JOHN ROMEYN BRODHEAD, A.M., LL.D.	New York, N.Y.	Died 6 May, 1873.

1 November, 1854.

BERNARD BEMIS WHITTEMORE, A.B.	Nashua, N.H.	
JOHN WADDINGTON, D.D. . .	London, Eng. .	Died 30 September, 1880.

6 December, 1854.

JOSEPH LEEDS.	Philadelphia, Pa.	Died 6 October, 1880.

3 January, 1855.

NAME.	RESIDENCE.	MEMBERSHIP CEASED.
HENRY TRUMAN BECKWITH . .	Providence, R. I.	Life Member, 1868.

7 March, 1855.

GEORGE FABER CLARK (Rev.) .	Norton . .	Elected Resident Member. 6 September, 1871.
GEORGE MOUNTFORT [1]	Canea, Candia .	Died 28 May, 1884.
WILLIAM RUDOLPH SMITH . .	Mineral Point, Wis.	Died 22 August, 1868.

4 April, 1855.

PISHEY THOMPSON	Boston, Lincoln. Eng.	Died 25 September, 1862.
JOSEPH EDMUND BULKLEY . .	New York, N. Y.	Died 3 November, 1879.
GEORGE HENRY MOORE, A.M., LL.D.	New York, N.Y.	Elected Honorary Member, 1 October, 1890.

2 May, 1855.

BRANTZ MAYER	Baltimore, Md.	Died 23 February, 1879.
JOHN SPEAR SMITH	Baltimore, Md.	Died 17 November, 1866.
WILLIAM BRADFORD REED, A.B., LL.D.	Philadelphia, Pa.	Died 18 February, 1876.
JOHN JORDAN, Jr.	Philadelphia, Pa.	Died 23 March, 1890.
WILLIAM DUANE.	Philadelphia, Pa.	Died 4 November, 1882.
TOWNSEND WARD	Philadelphia, Pa.	Died 13 August, 1885.
DAVID THOMAS VALENTINE .	New York, N.Y.	Died 25 February, 1869.

6 June, 1855.

WILLIAM ADEE WHITEHEAD, A.M.	Newark, N.J. .	Died 8 August, 1884.
SAMUEL HAYS CONGAR . . .	Newark, N.J. .	Died 29 July, 1872.
JOHN WAKEFIELD FRANCIS, M.D., LL.D.	New York, N Y.	Died 8 February, 1861.
GEORGE LONG DUYCKINCK, A.M.	New York, N.Y.	Died 30 March, 1863.
EVERT AUGUSTUS DUYCKINCK, A.M.	New York, N.Y.	Died 13 August, 1878.
WILLIAM CULLEN BRYANT, A.M., LL.D.	New York, N.Y.	Died 12 June, 1878.
THOMAS SMYTH, D.D.	Charleston, S.C.	Died 20 August, 1873.
GEORGE WASHINGTON BETHUNE, A.B., D.D.	Brooklyn, N.Y.	Died 28 April, 1862.

[1] About 1860 Mr. Mountfort returned to Boston, and became a Resident Member under Article 14 of the By-Laws adopted 3 October, 1855. The date of his becoming such does not appear; but the Corresponding Secretary reported to the Society, 6 August, 1862, the receipt of letters from the Rev. Henry Martyn Dexter (elected 2 July, 1862) and Mr. Mountfort, accepting Resident Membership. *Society's Records,* III. 155. See Resident Roll, 2 July, 1862.

Name.	Residence.	Membership ceased.
Henry Harbaugh (Rev.) . .	Lancaster, Pa. .	Died 28 December, 1867.
Samuel Irenæus Prime, A.B., D.D.	New York, N.Y.	Died 11 July, 1885.
Robert Mayo, M.D.	Washington, D.C.	Died 20 October, 1864.
Aaron Clark, A.M.	New York, N.Y.	Died 2 August, 1861.
Eben Goodwin	New York, N.Y.	Died 9 September, 1877.

1 August, 1855.

Winthrop Sargent, A.M., LL.B.	Philadelphia, Pa.	Died 18 May, 1870.
Thomas Wells Bartley, A.M.	Mansfield, Ohio	Died 20 June, 1885.

5 September, 1855.

Hovey Kilburn Clarke . . .	Detroit, Mich. .	Died 21 July, 1889.
Cyrus Woodman, A.M. . . .	Mineral Point, Wis.	Elected Resident Member, 6 February, 1867.
Peter Cooper, S.D., LL.D. .	New York, N.Y.	Died 4 April, 1883.
Ebenezer Meriam	Brooklyn, N.Y.	Died 19 March, 1864.
Henry Washington Lee, A.M., D.D., LL.D.	Davenport, Iowa	Died 26 September, 1874.

3 October, 1855.

John Lauris Blake, A.M., D.D.	Orange, N.J. .	Died 6 July, 1857.
Addison Kingsbury, D.D. . .	Putnam, Ohio .	Died 25 January, 1892.

7 November, 1855.

Elijah Middlebrook Haines .	Waukegan, Ill.	Died 25 April, 1889.
Samuel Hopkins Emery, A.M., D.D.	Quincy, Ill. . .	Elected Resident Member, 1 February, 1882.
Joseph Jackson Howard, LL.B., LL.D., F.S.A.	Blackheath, Kent, Eng.	

5 December, 1855.

Two Stickney	Toledo, Ohio .	Died 9 July, 1862.
Fordyce Mitchell Hubbard, D.D.	Chapel Hill, N.C.	Died 1 September, 1888.
Emanuel Vogel Gerhart, A.M., D.D., LL.D.	Lancaster, Pa.	

2 April, 1856.

William Williams Mather, A.M., LL.D.	Columbus, Ohio	Died 26 February, 1859.

7 May, 1856.

George Anson Dudley . . .	Ellenville, N.Y.	Died 3 March, 1886.

4 June, 1856.

NAME.	RESIDENCE.	MEMBERSHIP CEASED.
HENRY ADAMS (Rev.), A. M.	Peoria, Ill. . .	Died 27 March, 1883.

6 August, 1856.

CHARLES EDWARD LEVERETT McPherson, S.C. Died 30 November, 1868.
(Rev.), A. M.

3 September, 1856.

EBENEZER LANE, A. M., LL.D. . Chicago, Ill.　. Died 12 June, 1866.

5 November, 1856.

JOHN FREDERICK SCHROEDER, Brooklyn, N. Y. Died 26 February, 1857.
A. M., D. D.
WILLIAM DUDLEY, Jr. . . . . Madison, Wis. . Died 2 July, 1879.

3 December, 1856.

RICHARD SIMS　　. . . . London, Eng.

7 January, 1857.

WILLIAM BACHE　. . . . . Bristol, Pa.

4 February, 1857.

EDWIN DAWSON BUCKMAN, M.D. Bristol, Pa.　　Died 22 May, 1891.

4 March, 1857.

WILLIAM PAVER .　. . . . York, Eng. .　Died 1 July, 1871.

6 May, 1857.

JAMES BARDWELL RICHARDS, Harlem, N. Y. . Died 14 February, 1886.
A. M.

3 June, 1857.

JOEL MUNSELL . . . . . . Albany, N. Y. . Life Member, 1864.
　　　　　　　　　　　　　　　　　　　Died 15 January, 1880.
SAMUEL AUSTIN ALLIBONE, A. M., Philadelphia, Pa. Died 2 September, 1889.
LL. D.

1 July, 1857.

SAMUEL RUGGLES SLACK (Rev.) NEWARK, N. J. Elected Resident Mem-
　　　　　　　　　　　　　　　　　　　ber, 1 December, 1869.
ELI FRENCH, A. M. . . . . . New York, N. Y. Died 21 July, 1868.

5 August, 1857.

Name.	Residence.	Membership ceased.
Salomon Alofsen	Jersey City, N. J.	Life Member, 1865.
		Died 19 October, 1876.

2 September, 1857.

Henry Mitchell Smith, M. D.	New York, N. Y.	

4 November, 1857.

Henry Delavan Paine, M. D. .	Albany, N. Y.	
John Lauris Blake, A. M. . .	Orange, N. J.	
Reuben Hyde Walworth, LL. D.	Saratoga Springs, N. Y.	Elected Honorary Member, 2 August, 1865.

2 December, 1857.

Frederic Palmer Tracy (Rev.)	San Francisco, Cal.	See Resident Roll, 21 January, 1845. Died 9 October, 1860.
Francis Alfred Fabens, A. B., LL. B.	San Francisco, Cal.	Died 16 June, 1872.
William Jackson Davis . .	New York, N. Y.	Died 26 March, 1864.
John Allister McAllister .	Philadelphia, Pa.	

6 January, 1858.

William Meade, A. B., D. D. .	Millwood, Va. .	Died 14 March, 1862.
Samuel Osgood, A. M., D. D., LL. D.	New York, N. Y.	Died 14 April, 1880.
Frederic De Peyster, A. M., LL. D.	New York, N. Y.	Died 18 August, 1882.
Thomas De Witt, A. M., D. D. .	New York, N. Y.	Died 18 May, 1874.
Henry Theodore Tuckerman, A. M.	New York, N. Y.	Died 17 December, 1871.
William Darlington, M. D., LL. D.	West Chester, Pa.	Died 23 April, 1863.
Griffith John McRee, A. M. .	Wilmington, N.C.	Died 23 April, 1872.
Andrew Fuller Crane . . .	Baltimore, Md.	Died 11 January, 1885.
Edward Peacock, F. S. A. . .	Brigg, Lincoln, Eng.	
Robert Townsend	Albany, N. Y. .	Died 15 August, 1866.

3 February, 1858.

Luther Bradish, A. B., LL. D.	New York, N. Y.	Died 30 August, 1863.
Edward Robinson, A. M., D.D., LL. D.	New York, N. Y.	Died 27 January, 1863.

Name.	Residence.	Membership ceased.
Henry Steele Clarke, A.B., D.D.	Philadelphia, Pa.	Died 17 January, 1864.
Matthew Newkirk	Philadelphia, Pa.	Died 31 May. 1868.
David McKenney, A.B., D.D.	Pittsburg, Pa. .	Died 28 May, 1879.
Henry Chandler Bowen . .	New York, N.Y.	
Elam Smalley, A.B., D.D. .	Troy, N.Y. . .	Died 30 July, 1858.
Francis Brinley Fogg . . .	Nashville, Tenn.	Died 13 April, 1880.
Francis William Brinley . .	Perth Amboy,N.J.	Died 14 May, 1859.
Joseph Bradley Varnum, Jr., A.M.	New York, N.Y.	Died 31 December, 1874.
Albigence Waldo Putnam, A.B.	Nashville,Tenn.	Died 20 January, 1869.

3 March, 1858.

John Dickson Bruns, A.M., M.D.	Charleston, S.C.	Died 20 May, 1883.

7 April, 1858.

John Bostwick Moreau . .	New York, N.Y.	Died 10 March, 1886.
James Carson Brevoort, C.E., LL.D.	Brooklyn, N.Y.	Died 7 December, 1887.

5 May, 1858.

William Henry Tuthill . .	Tipton, Iowa .	Died 8 September, 1880.

2 June, 1858.

William Henry Kelley .	St. Paul, Minn.	See Resident Roll, 4 November, 1845.

1 September, 1858.

Edward Eaton Bowen . . .	New York, N.Y.	Died 14 March, 1887.
William Henry Allen, M.D., LL.D.	Philadelphia, Pa.	Died 27 August, 1882.
Benjamin Peter Hunt . .	Philadelphia, Pa.	Died 2 February, 1877.

6 October, 1858.

Joseph Green Cogswell, A.M., Ph.D., LL.D.	New York, N.Y.	Died 26 November, 1871.
Stephen Buttrick Noyes, A.B.	Brooklyn, N.Y.	Died 8 March, 1885.
Charles Combault Moreau	New York, N.Y.	
Alexandre Vattemare . . .	Paris, France .	Died 7 April, 1864.
John McAllister	Philadelphia, Pa.	Died 17 December, 1877.
Richard Eddy, Jr., D.D. . .	Canton, N.Y. .	30 November, 1869.
Joseph Howe.	Halifax, N.S. .	Died 1 June, 1873.

3 November, 1858.

NAME.	RESIDENCE.	MEMBERSHIP CEASED.
SETH HASTINGS GRANT, A. M.	New York, N. Y.	
CHARLES BENJAMIN RICHARDSON	New York, N. Y.	31 December, 1885. See Resident Roll, 6 August, 1856.
JAMES SPEAR LORING . . .	Brooklyn, N. Y.	See Resident Roll, 6 February, 1845. Died 12 April, 1884.
HENRY BARTON DAWSON . .	White Plains, N. Y.	Resgd. 19 February, 1868.
DAVID HARTER	Crawfordsville, Ind.	

1 December, 1858.

JOHN WOOD	Quincy, Ill. . .	Died 4 June, 1880.
FRANK VOSE	Baton Rouge, La.	Died 25 February, 1860.
WILLIAM EDWARD WARREN . .	Newburg, N. Y.	Died 13 January, 1877.

5 January, 1859.

JOSHUA SIDNEY HENSHAW . .	Utica, N. Y. .	Died 29 April, 1859.
WILLIAM EDWIN JOHNSTON, M.D.	Paris, France .	Died 15 February, 1886.

2 February, 1859.

CHARLES IRA BUSHNELL . . .	New York, N. Y.	Died 17 September, 1880.
CHARLES HARLEY CLEAVELAND, M.D.	Cincinnati, Ohio	Died 1 December, 1863.
DANIEL STEELE DURRIE, A. M. .	Madison, Wis.	
JOHN GILMARY SHEA,[1] LL. D. .	New York, N. Y.	Elected Honorary Member 1 October, 1890.
CHARLES DEXTER CLEVELAND, A. M., LL. D.	Philadelphia, Pa.	Died 18 August, 1869.
JAMES BERTRAND PAYEN-PAYNE, D. C. L., F. R. S. L., F. R. G. S., M. R. I. A.	South Kensington, London, Eng.	
JOHN STANFORD HOLME, A. B., D. D.	Brooklyn, N. Y.	Died 26 August, 1884.

2 March, 1859.

EBEN SPERRY STEARNS, A. M., D. D., LL. D.	Albany, N. Y. .	1 January, 1868. See Resident Roll, 7 July, 1852.
BENJAMIN POMEROY	New York, N. Y.	Died 28 December, 1866.

[1] Dr. Shea was baptized John Dawson Shea, but changed his name to John Gilmary Shea.

14

6 April, 1859.

NAME.	RESIDENCE.	MEMBERSHIP CEASED.

Isaac John Greenwood, Jr.,   New York, N. Y.
A.M.

1 June, 1859.

John Watts De Peyster, A.M.,   Tivoli, N. Y.
LL.D.

Thomas Bradlee . . . . .   Jamaica, N. Y.   Died 19 February, 1878.
George Washington Burnap,   Baltimore, Md.   Died 8 September, 1859.
A.M., D.D.

6 July, 1859.

Israel Keech Tefft . . . .   Savannah, Ga. .   Died 30 June, 1862.
Orlando Williams Wight, M.D. Rye, N. Y. . .   Died 19 October, 1888.
Samuel Trowbridge Champney Brooklyn, N. Y.   Died 21 October, 1885.
William Greenleaf Eliot, A.B., St. Louis, Mo. .   Died 23 January, 1887.
D.D.
Edwin Hubbell Chapin, A.M., New York, N. Y. Died 26 December, 1880.
D.D., LL.D.
Alexander Hamilton Vinton, Philadelphia, Pa. Elected Resident Mem-
A.M., M.D., D.D.   ber, 1 March, 1871.
Henry Whitney Bellows, A.B., New York, N. Y. Died 30 January, 1882.
D.D.
John Tuckett . . . . . .   London, Eng.
James Madison Porter . . . Easton, Pa. . .   Died 11 November, 1862.
John Stanwood Pulsifer . . Orwigsburgh, Pa. Died 6 September, 1866.
John Alsop King . . . . . Jamaica, N. Y.   Died 7 July, 1867.
Theodore Dwight . . . . . Brooklyn, N. Y.   Died 16 October, 1866.

3 August, 1859.

Return Jonathan Meigs, Jr. . Nashville, Tenn.
George Washington Hosmer, Buffalo, N. Y. . October, 1873.
A.M., D.D.
John Healy Heywood (Rev.), Louisville, Ky. 1 December, 1880.
A.B., D.D.
Thomas James Mumford (Rev.) Detroit, Mich. . 30 November, 1869.
Horatio Nelson Otis . . . New York, N. Y. Died 7 May, 1881.
Samuel Clarke Perkins, A.M., Philadelphia, Pa.
LL.B., LL.D.
Henry Ward Beecher (Rev.), Brooklyn, N. Y. Died 8 March, 1887.
A.B.
Octavius Brooks Frothingham New York, N. Y. 31 December, 1881.
(Rev.), A.M.
Amory Dwight Mayo (Rev.) . Albany, N. Y. . July, 1872.

Name.	Residence.	Membership ceased.
John Cordner (Rev.), LL. D.	Montreal, Can.	31 December, 1881. Elected Resident Member, 4 December. 1889.
David Masson, M. A., LL. D.	London, Eng.	Elected Honorary Member, 1 October, 1890.
Henry Longueville Mansel, M.A.. D. D., LL. D.	Oxford, Eng.	Died 31 July, 1871.
Richard Chenevix Trench, M.A., D.D.	London, Eng.	Died 28 March, 1886.
Samuel Longfellow (Rev.). A.B.	Brooklyn, N. Y.	31 December, 1861.
Abiel Abbot Livermore, A.M., D. D.	Yonkers, N. Y.	
Hiram Parker Crozier (Rev.)	New York, N. Y.	Died 6 March, 1883.
William Henry Furness, A.M., D. D.	Philadelphia, Pa.	
Oliver Stearns, A. M., D.D.	Meadville, Pa.	30 November, 1869.
George Henry Jerome	Iowa City. Iowa	Died 15 August, 1886.
Horatio Gates Somerby	London, Eng.	See Resident Roll, 7 March, 1845. Died 14 November, 1872.
Frederick Augustus Farley, A. M., D.D.	Brooklyn, N.Y.	Died 24 March, 1892.

5 October, 1859.

Franklin Chase	Tampico, Mexico.	Died 27 December, 1890.

2 November, 1859.

William Mason Cornell. A.M., M.D., D.D., LL. D.	Philadelphia, Pa.	30 November, 1869. See Resident Roll, 6 February. 1856, and 1 December, 1869.
Ebenezer Cyril Arnold	Milwaukee. Wis.	May, 1876.
Henry Reed Stiles, A. M., M. D.	Brooklyn, N. Y.	
Alexander Augustus Smets	Savannah, Ga.	Died 9 May, 1862.

7 December, 1859.

Edwin Augustine Dalrymple, D.D.	Baltimore. Md.	Elected Honorary Member, 7 October, 1863.
Jacob Gilbert Forman (Rev.), LL. B.	Alton. Ill.	30 November, 1869.
William Thomas Smithett, A.M., D. D.	Galesburg, Ill.	See Resident Roll, 3 February, 1858. Died 24 March, 1888.

NAME.	RESIDENCE.	MEMBERSHIP CEASED.
JOSEPH BLACKBURNE BOND, M.D.	Yarmouth, N.S.	Died 18 September, 1882.
ISAAC SMITH HOMANS	New York, N.Y.	Died 27 May, 1874.

4 January, 1860.

AMOS DEAN, A.B., LL.D. . .	Albany, N.Y. .	Died 26 January, 1868.
WILLIAM NOËL SAINSBURY . .	London, Eng.	

1 February, 1860.

ALBERT BARNES (Rev.), A.B. .	Philadelphia, Pa.	Died 24 December, 1870.
FRANKLIN BENJAMIN HOUGH, A.B., M.D., LL.D.	Albany, N.Y. .	Died 11 June, 1885.

15 February, 1860.

HENRY MARTYN FIELD, A.M., D.D.	New York, N.Y.	

7 March, 1860.

GEORGE LOVELL CARY, A.M. .	Yellow Springs, Ohio.	
HENRY FLANDERS, A.M. . . .	Philadelphia, Pa.	

4 April, 1860.

NATHAN HENRY CHAMBERLAIN (Rev.), A.B.	Baltimore, Md.	31 December 1863. See Resident Roll, 3 December, 1856.
THOMAS OSBORNE RICE (Rev.), A.M.	Charleston, S.C.	30 November, 1869. See Resident Roll, 2 March, 1859.
GEORGE WILLIAM BAGBY, M.D.	Richmond, Va. .	Died 29 November, 1883.
JAMES DUNCAN GRAHAM, U.S.A.	Chicago, Ill. . .	Died 28 December, 1865.

2 May, 1860.

JAMES SMITH BUCK	Milwaukee, Wis.	

6 June, 1860.

CHARLES JAMES BOWEN (Rev.), A.B.	Baltimore, Md.	30 November, 1869.
STEPHEN VAUGHN SHIPMAN . .	Madison, Wis.	

11 July, 1860.

FRANK MOORE, A.M.	New York, N.Y.	
DAVID LOWRY SWAIN, LL.D. .	Chapel Hill, N.C.	Died 27 August, 1868.

1 August, 1860.

Name.	Residence.	Membership ceased.
Nicholas Esterhazy Stephen Armytage Hamilton	London, Eng.	
Robert Lemon, F.S.A. . . .	London, Eng. .	Died 3 January. 1867.
Carl Christian Rafn, Ph. D., J. U. D., F.S.A., F.R.G.S., R.S.N.A.	Copenhagen, Den.	Died 20 October. 1864.

5 September, 1860.

George Goundry Munger, A.B.	Rochester, N.Y.	
Martyn Paine, A.M., M.D., LL.D.	New York, N.Y.	Died 10 November, 1877.

3 October, 1860.

Sir Louis Hypolite La Fontaine, Bart.	Montreal, Can.	Died 26 February, 1864.
Thomas Hicks Wynne . . .	Richmond, Va. .	Died 24 February, 1875.
Charles Campbell, A.B. . .	Petersburg, Va.	Died 11 July, 1876.
Rufus Richardson Belknap .	Brooklyn, N.Y.	Died 5 March, 1878.

7 November, 1860.

James Humphrey	Brooklyn. N.Y.	Died 16 June, 1866.
Thomas Hughes, F.S.A. . . .	Chester, Eng. .	Died 30 May. 1890.
Increase Allen Lapham, LL.D.	Milwaukee, Wis.	Died 14 September, 1875.

5 December, 1860.

Henry Adolphus Miles, A.M., D.D.	Florence, Italy .	30 November. 1869. See Resident Roll, 2 December, 1857.

19 December, 1860.

Calvin Fletcher, A.M. . .	Indianapolis, Ind.	Life Member. 1861. Died 26 March, 1866.
Eliab Kingman, A.M. . .	Washington, D.C.	Died 1 February, 1883.

2 January, 1861.

Addison Weld Champney . .	New York, N.Y.	Died 22 October, 1876.

16 January, 1861.

John Jay Smith	Germantown, Pa.	Died 23 September, 1881.

6 February, 1861.

Alfred Greenleaf, A.M. . .	Brooklyn. N.Y.	Died 26 December, 1872.
Edward Burgess	Poughkeepsie, N.Y.	

6 March, 1861.

NAME.	RESIDENCE.	MEMBERSHIP CEASED.
JARVIS MALATIAH HATCH . .	Rochester, N. Y.	Died 11 August, 1862.
BENJAMIN HOMER HALL . . .	Troy, N. Y.	
JAMES RIKER	New York, N. Y.	Died 3 July, 1889.
BERIAH BOTFIELD, M.A., F.R.S,	Daventry,	Died 7 August, 1863.
F.S.A., F.G.S., F.L.S., F.R.A.S.,	Northampton, Eng.	
M. R. I. A.		
ISRAEL DANIEL RUPP	Philadelphia, Pa.	Died 31 May, 1878.

1 May, 1861.

JOHN MEIGS	Nashville, Tenn.	
MATTHEW SCHROPP HENRY . .	Philadelphia, Pa.	Died 20 January, 1862.
EPHRAIM GEORGE SQUIER, A. M.	New York, N. Y.	Died 17 April, 1888.

5 June, 1861.

WILLIAM EWING DU BOIS . .	Philadelphia, Pa.	Died 14 July, 1881.
HENRY ONDERDONK, Jr., A.B. .	Jamaica, N. Y. .	Died 24 June, 1886.
RICHARD STEPHEN CHARNOCK,	London, Eng.	
M. A., Ph. D., F. S. A.		

3 July, 1861.

DANIEL HENSHAW, A. M. .	Lisbon, Wis. .	See Resident Roll, 7 October, 1857. Died 9 July, 1863.
WILLIAM WINTHROP	Valetta, Malta .	Died 3 July, 1869.
CLIFFORD STANLEY SIMS . .	Philadelphia, Pa.	
GREGGS JOSEPH FARISH .	Yarmouth, N. S.	Died 19 December, 1881.

7 August, 1861.

THOMAS SPOONER . . .	Reading, Ohio .	Life Member, 1865. Died 10 March, 1890.

4 September, 1861.

JAMES CARNAHAN WETMORE .	Columbus, Ohio.	
THOMAS HUGHES, B. A. . .	London, Eng.	

2 October, 1861.

GEORGE HERRIOT TUCKER, M.D.	New York, N.Y.	Died 25 January, 1862.
FREDERIC AUGUSTUS HOLDEN .	Washington, D.C.	
JOHN REYNOLDS	Belleville, Ill. .	Died 8 May, 1865.
GILBERT COPE	West Chester, Pa.	

6 November, 1861.

NAME.	RESIDENCE.	MEMBERSHIP CEASED.
JOHN HOWARD REDFIELD . .	Philadelphia, Pa.	
THOMAS WRIGHT, M.A., F.S.A.	London, Eng. .	Died 23 December, 1877.
ROBERT PATTERSON DU BOIS, A.M., D.D.	New London, Pa.	Died 21 February, 1882.

5 February, 1862.

DAVID HARLOW PEASE . . .	Norwalk, Ohio .	Died 13 January, 1872.
GEORGE KENT, A.M.	Valencia, Spain	30 November, 1869.

5 March, 1862.

GEORGE GROUT HAPGOOD, A.M., D.D.	Boonville, N.Y.	Died 17 May, 1876.

3 September, 1862.

WILLIAM TURNER COGGESHALL .	Springfield, Ohio	Died 2 August, 1867.

1 October, 1862.

NAPOLEON BONAPARTE MOUNT-FORT	New York, N.Y.	Died 22 November, 1883.
JOSEPH LEMUEL CHESTER, D.C.L., LL.D.	London, Eng. .	Died 26 May, 1882.

5 November, 1862.

HENRY MAINE	Brooklyn, N.Y.	

7 January, 1863.

GEORGE SMITH, M.D.	Upper Darby, Pa.	Died 10 March, 1882.

4 March, 1863.

CHARLES BRECK, A.M., D.D.	Wilmington, Del.	Died 12 June, 1891.

1 April, 1863.

FREDERIC BEECHER PERKINS, A.M.	New York, N.Y.	Elected Resident Member, 5 February, 1873.

6 May, 1863.

CHARLES GODFREY LELAND, A.M., F.R.S.L.	Philadelphia, Pa.	

3 June, 1863.

JOHN SMITH FUTHEY	West Chester, Pa.	Died 26 November, 1888.

1 July, 1863.

NAME.	RESIDENCE.	MEMBERSHIP CEASED.
JOHN AUSTIN STEVENS, Jr., A.B.	New York, N.Y.	

5 August, 1863.

BENJAMIN HOMER DIXON . . .	Toronto, Can. .	See Resident Roll, 6 February, 1850.

2 September, 1863.

MARTIN BOWEN SCOTT . . .	Cleveland, Ohio	Died 2 February, 1872.

7 October, 1863.

BUCKINGHAM SMITH,[1] LL.B. .	New York, N.Y.	Died 6 January, 1871.

4 November, 1863.

WILLIAM MARTIN WILSON . .	Greenville, Ohio	Died 15 June, 1864.
GEORGE PURNELL FISHER, A.B.	Dover, Del.	

2 December, 1863.

FREEMAN HARLOW MORSE . .	London, Eng. .	Died 6 February, 1891.

3 February, 1864.

FRANCIS SAMUEL DRAKE . . .	Leavenworth, Kan.	31 December, 1870. See Resident Roll, 3 February, 1858.
ALDEN JERMAIN SPOONER . .	Brooklyn, N.Y.	Died 2 August, 1881.

2 March, 1864.

JOHN BEARSE NEWCOMB . . .	Elgin, Ill.	

6 April, 1864.

JAMES DEAN FISH	New York, N.Y.	3 December, 1889.

4 May, 1864.

JOSEPH HARTWELL BARRETT, A.M.	Washington, D.C.	

6 July, 1864.

JOHN GOUGH NICHOLS, F.S.A. .	London, Eng. .	Died 14 November, 1873.

---

[1] Mr. Smith's original name was Thomas Buckingham Smith.

3 August, 1864.

7 September, 1864.

5 October, 1864.

2 November, 1864.

7 December, 1864.

4 January, 1865.

5 April, 1865.

2 August, 1865.

1 November, 1865.

7 February, 1866.

4 April, 1866.

1 August, 1866.

5 September, 1866.

7 November, 1866.

Name.	Residence.	Membership ceased.
George Rogers Howell, A.M.	Southampton, N.Y.	

2 January, 1867.

William Smith Ellis . . . . Charlwood, Surrey, Eng.   Died 22 March, 1890.

6 March, 1867.

John Patrick Prendergast, B.A.   Dublin, Ireland.

5 June, 1867.

Joseph Farrand Tuttle, A.M., D.D., LL.D.   Crawfordsville, Ind.

3 July, 1867.

John Meredith Read, Jr., A.M., LL.B., F.S.A., F.R.G.S., M.R.I.A.   Albany, N.Y.

7 August, 1867.

Stephen Whitney Phœnix, A.M., LL.B.   New York, N.Y.   Died 3 November, 1831.

2 October, 1867.

Benjamin Scott, F.R.A.S. . .   London, Eng.   Died 17 January, 1892.

6 November, 1867.

Jacob M Da Costa,[1] A.M., M.D., LL.D.   Philadelphia, Pa.

4 December, 1867.

Henry Augustus Homes (Rev.), A.M., LL.D.   Albany, N.Y. . .   Died 3 November, 1887.

5 February, 1868.

Beamish Murdoch, D.C.L. . .   Halifax, N.S. . .   Died 9 February, 1876.

4 March, 1868.

Austin Wells Holden, A.M., M.D.   Glens Falls, N.Y.   Died 19 July, 1891.

6 May, 1868.

Benjamin Parke, LL.D. . .   Hopbottom, Pa.   Died 29 May, 1882.

[1] Dr. Da Costa has no middle name, but uses "M" as a designation.

2 September, 1868.

NAME.	RESIDENCE.	MEMBERSHIP CEASED.
OSGOOD FIELD, F.S.A. . . .	London, Eng.	
GEORGE WOLFF FAHNESTOCK .	Philadelphia, Pa.	Life Member, 1868.
		Died 3 December, 1868.

2 December, 1868.

ELIHU OLIVER LYMAN . . . . Mulberry Corners, Ohio.

6 January, 1869.

JONATHAN TENNEY, A.M., Ph.D. Albany, N.Y. . See Resident Roll, 2 September, 1863. Died 24 February, 1888.

3 February, 1869.

FRANCIS SOUTHACK HOYT, A.M., Delaware, Ohio.
D.D.

6 October, 1869.

ROBERT CLARKE . . . . . . Cincinnati, Ohio.

3 November, 1869.

CHARLES CANDEE BALDWIN, A.M., Cleveland, Ohio.
LL.B.

2 March, 1870.

CONRAD ENGELHARDT, R.S.N.A. Copenhagen, Den. Died 11 November, 1881.

6 April, 1870.

BENJAMIN WOODBRIDGE DWIGHT Clinton, N.Y. . Died 18 September, 1889.
(Rev.), A.B., Ph.D., LL.D.

1 June, 1870.

LYMAN COLEMAN, A.M., D.D. . Easton, Pa. . . Died 16 March, 1882.

5 October, 1870.

ROBERT WILLIAM HARRIS, A.M., Astoria, N.Y. . Died 5 December, 1886.
D.D.

7 December, 1870.

NELSON SLATER (Rev.), A.M. .	Sacramento. Cal.	Died 9 May. 1886.
CHARLES PERRIN SMITH . . .	Trenton. N.J. .	Died 17 January, 1883.
WILLIAM JOHNSON BACON, A.M., LL.D.	Utica, N.Y. .	Died 3 July, 1889.
ROBERT SAFFORD HALE, A.B., LL.D.	Elizabethtown, N.Y.	Died 14 December, 1881.

4 January, 1871.

NAME.	RESIDENCE.	MEMBERSHIP CEASED.

WILLIAM INGRAHAM KIP, A.M.,   San Francisco,
D.D., LL.D.   Cal.

7 June, 1871.

JAMES ROSS SNOWDEN, A.M.   . Philadelphia, Pa. Died 21 March, 1878.

4 October, 1871.

ALFRED SANDHAM . . . . . Montreal, Can.

3 January, 1872.

GEORGE WASHINGTON PORTER, Port Leyden, N.Y. 31 December, 1879.
D.D.

7 February, 1872.

BENJAMIN FRANKLIN DE COSTA, New York, N.Y. See Resident Roll,
D.D.   1 June, 1864.

6 March, 1872.

JOHN LEE WATSON, U.S.N., Orange, N.J. . See Resident Roll,
A.M., D.D.   2 September, 1868.
                                           Died 12 August, 1884.

5 June, 1872.

TRUMAN HENRY SAFFORD, A.B., Chicago, Ill. . 31 December, 1876.
Ph.D.

2 October, 1872.

JOHN FLETCHER WILLIAMS, S.B. St. Paul, Minn.

1 January, 1873.

JOHN BROOKS RUSSELL [1] . . . Washington, D.C. Died 11 March, 1891.

5 February, 1873.

WILLIAM STEVENS PERRY, A.M., Geneva, N.Y.
D.D., D.C.L., LL.D.

5 March, 1873.

JOHN JORDAN LATTING, A.M. . New York, N.Y. Died 16 December, 1890.

2 April, 1873.

JAMES SEYMOUR GRINNELL, A.M. Washington, D.C. 10 February, 1877.
                                           Elected Resident Member, 4 December, 1889.

[1] Mr. Russell's name was changed (in 1819) from John Russell Estabrooks.

4 June, 1873.

NAME.	RESIDENCE.	MEMBERSHIP CEASED.
JOHN RANDOLPH BRYAN	Columbia, Va.	Died 13 September, 1887.

3 September, 1873.

CHARLES HUGHES . . . . . Montreal, Can.

3 December, 1873.

CHARLES ROGERS (Rev.), LL.D. Forest Hill,   Died 18 September, 1890.
Surrey, Eng.

4 March, 1874.

WILLIAM JOHN POTTS . . . . Camden, N.J.

6 May, 1874.

HORACE EDWIN HAYDEN (Rev.), Brownsville, Pa.
A.M.

3 June, 1874.

FOXHALL ALEXANDER PARKER, Annapolis, Md.   Died 10 June, 1879.
U.S.N.

2 September, 1874.

GEORGE BEATSON BLENKIN (Rev.), Boston, Lincoln, Died 21 February, 1892.
M.A.   Eng.

4 November. 1874.

FREDERICK BROWN (Rev.), M.A., Beckenham,   Died 11 March, 1886.
F.S.A.   Kent, Eng.

2 December, 1874.

JOHN ADAMS DIX, U.S.A., Albany, N.Y. . Died 21 April, 1879.
A.M., LL.D.

6 January, 1875.

GEORGE HERBERT PATTERSON Suspension Bridge, 1 December, 1883.
(Rev.), A.M., LL.B.   N.Y.   Elected Resident Member, 4 December, 1889.

3 March, 1875.

ISAAC FRANCIS WOOD, A.B. . . New York, N.Y.

7 April, 1875.

GIDEON DELAPLAINE SCULL . . Hounslow Heath, Died 22 April, 1889.
London, Eng.

2 June, 1875.

NAME.	RESIDENCE.	MEMBERSHIP CEASED.
DANIEL RAVENEL	Charleston, S.C.	
ROBERT ALONZO BROCK . . .	Richmond, Va.	

9 October, 1875.

JAMES MACPHERSON LE MOINE, Quebec, Can. . Elected Honorary Mem-
F.R.S.C. ber, 1 October, 1890.

3 November, 1875.

AUGUSTUS WHITTEMORE CORLISS, Camp McDowell,
U.S.A. Arizona.

1 December, 1875.

L'Abbé HENRI RAYMOND CAS- Rivière Ouelle,
GRAIN, D. Litt., F.R.S.C. Can.

5 January, 1876.

HERVEY CHARLES PECHELL . . Maresfield Park,
Sussex, Eng.

1 March, 1876.

CHARLES TRELAWNY COLLINS Ham, Plymouth, Died 19 April, 1878.
TRELAWNY (Rev.), M.A. Eng.
JOHN SCRIBNER JENNESS, A.B. New York, N.Y. Died 10 August, 1879.

3 May, 1876.

DIVIE BETHUNE McCARTEE, A.M., Tokio, Japan.
M.D.

7 June, 1876.

JOSEPH ANDRÉ CASIMIR CONTÉ Marseilles,
France.
SPENCER BONSALL . . . . . Philadelphia, Pa. Died 4 April, 1888.

4 October, 1876.

ALEXANDER GREGG, A.M., D.D., Galveston, Tex.
LL.D.

1 November, 1876.

GEORGE ARCHIE STOCKWELL. Port Huron,
A.M., Ph.D., M.D., F.Z.S. Mich.

6 December, 1876.

WILLIAM GILBERT DAVIES, A.M., New York, N.Y.
S.B.

[1] Mr. Hildeburn's original name was Charles Swift Riché Hildeburn.

1 May, 1878.

NAME.   RESIDENCE.   MEMBERSHIP CEASED.

Sir GILBERT EDWARD CAMPBELL, Ballyshannon,
  Bart.   Donegal, Ireland.

5 June, 1878.

GEORGE HERBERT LEE, M.A.,   St. John, N. B.
  B. C. L.

2 October, 1878.

GEORGE DOUGLAS MILLER, A. B.   New Brighton,
                         N. Y.

6 November, 1878.

MOSES HALE WILDER (Rev.)   .   Brooklyn, N.Y.   Died 11 November, 1879.

4 December, 1878.

GEORGE ALFRED RAIKES, F.S.A.,   Hampstead,
  F.S.S., F.R.S.L.   London, Eng.

5 February, 1879.

WILLIAM DEAN . . . . . .   West Kensington,
                         London, Eng.

5 March, 1879.

MOSES HARVEY (Rev.), B. A.,   St. John's, N. F.
  LL.D., F.R.G.S., F.R.S.C.

7 May, 1879.

SAMUEL CHENERY DAMON, A.B.,   Honolulu, H.I. . Died 7 February, 1885.
  D.D.

1 October, 1879.

ROSWELL RANDALL HOES (Rev.),   New Rochelle,
  U.S.N., A.M.   N.Y.

5 November, 1879.

JOSÉ ANTONIO DE LAVALLE,   Quebec, Can. . Died 17 October, 1888.
  El Conde de Premio Real

7 January, 1880.

CHARLES MORRIS BLAKE (Rev.),   San Francisco,
  A.M., M.D.   Cal.

4 February, 1880.

3 March, 1880.

7 April, 1880.

5 May, 1880.

2 June, 1880.

1 September, 1880.

6 October, 1880.

3 November, 1880.

1 December, 1880.

5 January, 1881.

2 February, 1881.

2 March, 1881.

6 April, 1881.

NAME.	RESIDENCE.	MEMBERSHIP CEASED.
RICHARD SALTER STORRS, A.M., L.H.D., D.D., LL.D.	Brooklyn, N.Y.	

4 May, 1881.

JAMES BURRELL . . . . . . Central City, Col. Died 8 August, 1887.

1 June, 1881.

HENRY WASHINGTON BENHAM, U.S.A. — New York, N.Y. — See Resident Roll, 2 December, 1874. Died 30 May, 1884.

7 September, 1881.

CHARLES WELLS HAYES, A.M., D.D. — Westfield, N.Y. — See Resident Roll, 6 September, 1876.

5 October, 1881.

Mgr. ROBERT SETON, J.U.B., D.D., LL.D. — Jersey City, N.J.

2 November, 1881.

WILLIAM HENRY EGLE, A.M., M.D. — Harrisburg, Pa.

7 December, 1881.

CHARLES HENRY COOTE . . . London, Eng. .

4 January, 1882.

RALPH WOOD KENYON, A.M., D.B. — Brooklyn, N.Y. — See Resident Roll, 4 May, 1881.

1 February, 1882.

WILLIAM FREDERICK POOLE, A.M., LL.D. — Evanston, Ill. .

1 March, 1882.

JOSEPH HENRY STICKNEY . . Baltimore, Md.

5 April, 1882.

HORATIO HALE,[1] A.M., F.R.S.C. — Clinton, Can.

3 May, 1882.

CHARLES DANIEL DRAKE, LL.D. — Washington, D.C. Died 1 April, 1892.

[1] Mr. Hale's original name was Horatio Emmons Hale.

7 June, 1882.

6 September, 1882.

4 October, 1882.

1 November, 1882.

7 February, 1883.

7 March, 1883.

4 April, 1883.

2 May, 1883.

5 September, 1883.

3 October. 1883.

7 November, 1883.

5 December, 1883.

2 April, 1884.

NAME.	RESIDENCE.	MEMBERSHIP CEASED.
NATHANIEL HOLMES MORISON, A. M., LL. D.	Baltimore, Md.	Elected Honorary Member, 1 October, 1890.

7 May, 1884.

LEWIS HENRY STEINER, A. M., M. D., Litt. D., LL. D.	Frederick City, Md.	Died 18 February, 1892.

4 June, 1884.

Sir JOHN CAMPBELL ALLEN, LL. D.	Fredericton, N. B.	Elected Honorary Member, 1 October, 1890.

3 September, 1884.

CHARLES FRANKLIN ROBERTSON, A. M., D. D., LL. D.	St. Louis, Mo. .	Died 1 May, 1886.

1 October, 1884.

JOHN JAMES RAVEN, M. A., D. D.	Fressingfield, Suffolk, Eng.

5 November, 1884.

ASA BIRD GARDINER, U. S. A., A. M., LL. B., LL. D.	New York, N. Y.

3 December, 1884.

EDWARD EGGLESTON, A. M., D. D.	New York, N. Y.

7 January, 1885.

EDWARD AUGUSTUS FREEMAN, M. A., D. C. L., LL. D.	Wells, Somerset, Eng.	Elected Honorary Member, 1 October, 1890.

4 February, 1885.

CHARLES KENDALL ADAMS, A. M., LL. D.	Ann Arbor, Mich.	Elected Honorary Member, 1 October, 1890.

4 March, 1885.

JUSTIN McCARTHY, B. A. . .	London, Eng.

1 April, 1885.

Sir THEODORE MARTIN, K. C. B., LL. D.	Bath, Somerset, Eng.	Elected Honorary Member, 1 October, 1890.

6 May, 1885.

WILLIAM HARDEN	Savannah, Ga.

Name.	Residence.	Membership ceased.
Charles William Darling	. Utica, N. Y.	

October, 1885.

Francis Grigson	London, Eng. .	Died 25 September, 1886.

2 December, 1885.

Lyon Gardiner Tyler, A.M. .	Richmond, Va.

3 March, 1886.

David Sherwood Kellogg, A.M., Plattsburg, N. Y.
M.D.

7 April, 1886.

George Morgan Hills, A.M., Burlington, N. J. Died 15 October, 1890.
D. D.

2 June, 1886.

George Archibald Smith (Rev.), Alexandria, Va.   Died 28 June, 1889.
A. M.

1 September, 1886.

Charles Richmond Weld, D.B.   Baltimore, Md.

6 October, 1886.

John Henry Evans d'Oyley,   Paris, France .   Life Member, 1886.
Marquis d'Oyley, M.A.S., M.D.,
D. D. S.

3 November, 1886.

Charles Harold Evelyn White   Ipswich, Suffolk,
(Rev.), F.S.A.   Eng.

1 December, 1886.

James Anthony Froude, M.A.   London, Eng. .   Elected Honorary Member, 1 October, 1890.

5 January, 1887.

Cecil Hampden Cutts Howard   Brooklyn, N.Y.

4 May, 1887.

Henry Farnham Burke, F.S.A.   London, Eng.

1 June, 1887.

Ellsworth Eliot, A.M., M.D.   New York, N.Y.

7 September, 1887.

NAME.   RESIDENCE.   MEMBERSHIP CEASED.

GEORGE BOWN MILLETT, M.R.C.S., Penzance,
Cornwall, Eng.

2 November, 1887.

THOMAS MAXWELL POTTS . . . Canonsburg, Pa.

7 December, 1887.

ANDREW OLIVER, A.M., D.D. . New York, N.Y.

4 January, 1888.

VINCENZO PALIZZOLO GRAVINA, Palermo, Italy.
Baron de Ramione

4 April, 1888.

NICHOLAS DARNELL DAVIS . . Georgetown,
Demarara, B.G.

6 June, 1888.

JOHN EATON (Rev.), A.M., Ph.D., Marietta, Ohio.
LL. D.

3 October, 1888.

WILLIAM PHILLIMORE WATTS Chiswick,
PHILLIMORE, M.A., B.C.L.   Middlesex, Eng.

5 December, 1888.

JAMES ATKINS NOYES, A.B., Ph.B. New York, N.Y. Elected Resident Member 6 January, 1892.

2 January, 1889.

FRANCIS SMITH NASH, A.B., M.D. Washington, D.C.

Life Members not Resident Members.

HONORARY MEMBER.

Elected.		Name.	Residence.	L. M.
1847	January 6	James Brown Thornton . . .	Saco, Maine	1871

CORRESPONDING MEMBERS.

1845	February 6 .	Samuel Holden Parsons, A.M. .	Hartford, Conn. . .	1865
	November 4	Nathaniel Chauncey, A.M. . .	Philadelphia, Pa. . .	1862
1846	February 4 .	Ebenezer Alden, A.M., M.D. .	Randolph	1864
1847	May 5 . .	Samuel Dana Bell, A.B., LL.D.	Manchester, N. H. .	1863
1850	December 18	John Wentworth, A.M., LL.D. .	Chicago, Ill.	1865
1851	February 5 .	Edward Kidder	Wilmington, N. C.	1871
1855	January 3 .	Henry Truman Beckwith . . .	Providence, R. I. . .	1868
1857	June 3 . .	Joel Munsell . .	. .	Albany, N.Y. . . .	1864
	August 5 .	Salomon Alofsen	Jersey City, N. J. . .	1865
1860	December 19	Calvin Fletcher, A.M.	Indianapolis, Ind. . .	1861
1861	August 7 .	Thomas Spooner	Reading, Ohio . . .	1865
1866	August 1 .	Ledyard Bill	New York, N. Y. . .	1867
1868	September 2	George Wolff Fahnestock . .	Philadelphia, Pa. . .	1868
1886	October 6 .	John Henry Evans d'Oyley, Marquis d'Oyley, M.A.S., M.D., D.D.S.	Paris, France . . .	1886

Index of Officers.

Index of Members.

BALFOUR, David Miller, 54.
BALL, Abel, 31.
BALLARD, James Morton, 38.
Joseph, 20.
BALLISTER, Joseph Fennelly, 63.
BALLOU, Frederick Milton, 69.
Russell Arnold, 63.
BANCROFT, George, 81.
Sidney Capen, 39.
BARBOUR, John Nathaniel, 52.
BARKER, Edward Tobey, 35.
BARNARD, Henry, 93.
BARNES, Albert, 108.
William, 77.
BARR, George Lyman, 42.
BARRETT, Edwin Shepard, 57.
George Potter, 71.
James, 76.
Joseph Hartwell, 112.
William, 43.
BARROWS, Horace Granville, 17.
John Henry, 64.
Samuel June, 63.
William, 61.
BARRY, John Stetson, 11.
William, 94.
BARSTOW, John, 16.
Josiah Whitney, 53.
Zedekiah Smith, 96.
BARTLET, William Stoodley, 12.
BARTLETT, John Russell, 38.
Shubael, 99.
Thomas Edward, 60.
BARTLEY, Thomas Wells, 101.
BASSETT, Elisha, 49.
Francis, 40.
BATCHELDER, Samuel, 49.
Samuel, Jr., 23.
BATCHELLER, Alfred Hubbard, 46.
BATES, Benjamin Edward, 39.
Caleb, 3.
Isaac Chapman, 53.
Phineas, Jr., 56.
William, 19.
William Carver, 48.
BATTLES, Frank Forbes, 48.
James Monroe, 34.
BAURY, Alfred Louis, 95.
BAXTER, James Phinney, 66.
BAYLEY, Augustus Ramsay, 57.
BAYLIES, William, 93.
BEAL, Alexander, 13.
James Henry, 44.
BEAMAN, Charles Cotesworth, 56.

BEAN, Aaron Heywood, 45.
BEARD, Alanson Wilder, 54.
Ithamar Warren, 11.
BECKWITH, Henry Truman, 100, 127.
BEEBE, James Madison, 28.
BEECHER, Henry Ward, 106.
BEEDHAM, Braylesford Harry, 123.
BELKNAP, George Eugene, 63.
Rufus Richardson, 109.
BELL, Albert Decatur Spaulter, 43.
Alexander Graham, 77.
Charles Henry, 37.
Charles Upham, 73.
John James, 37.
John William, 67
Samuel Dana, 19, 94, 127.
BELLOWS, Henry Whitney, 106.
BEMIS, Charles Vose, 57.
BENEDICT, William Leonard, 76.
BENHAM, Henry Washington, 55, 122.
BENNETT, Edmund Hatch, 43, 79.
BENSON, Arthur Fitch, 79.
BENT, Samuel Tucker, 64.
Silas, 121.
BENTON, Austin Williams, 44.
BERRY, Abel Blanchard, 32.
BETHUNE, George Washington, 100.
BICKNELL, Quincy, 51.
Thomas Williams, 45.
William Emery, 31.
BIGELOW, Andrew, 5.
Frank Winthrop, 15.
George Brooks, 29.
Horatio Nelson, 14.
John, 35.
Timothy, 64.
BILL, Ledyard, 113, 127.
BILLINGS, Frederick, 76.
BINNEY, Charles James Fox, 6.
Horace, 86.
William Cushing, 97.
BISHOP, Joseph Pinckney Ponsonby, 68.
Robert Roberts, 66.
Thomas Wetmore, 80.
BLACK, James Wallace, 47.
BLAIKIE, Alexander, 13.
BLAKE, Arthur Welland, 71.
Charles Morris, 120.
Francis Everett, 50.
George Baty, 27.
John Harrison, 4.
John Lauris, 101, 103.
Mortimer, 97.
Pynson, 23.

BLAKE (Cont'd).
Samuel, 23.
Stanton, 60.
BLAKEMORE, John Eli, 79.
BLANCHARD, George Dana
Boardman, 14.
BLASLAND, Edward Boutelle, 72.
BLATCHFORD, Eliphalet Wickes, 38.
BLENKIN, George Beatson, 117.
BLISS, Cornelius Newton, 30.
Edward Penniman, 63.
Henry Penniman, 806.
Richard, Jr., 52.
Sylvester, 8.
BOARDMAN, Halsey Joseph, 29.
Samuel Lane, 53.
BODFISH, Joshua Peter, 57.
BODGE, George Madison, 55.
BOLTON, Charles Knowles, 76.
Robert, 113.
BOLTWOOD, Lucius Manlius, 92.
BOND, George William, 38.
Henry, 89.
Joseph Blackburne, 108.
BONSALL, Spencer, 118.
BORDEN, Nathaniel Briggs, 23.
BOSSON, Albert Davis, 80.
BOTFIELD, Beriah, 110.
BOURNE, Edward Emerson, 33.
BOUTELLE, John Alonzo, 13.
BOUTON, Nathaniel, 93.
BOUTWELL, Francis Marion, 59.
George Sewall, 68.
BOWDITCH, Charles Pickering, 64.
BOWDLEAR, William Augustus, 61.
BOWEN, Charles James, 108.
Edward Eaton, 104.
Henry Chandler, 104.
BOWERS, Dwight Eliot, 77.
BOWMAN, Selwin Zadock, 25.
BOYD, John, 56.
BOYDEN, Amos Josiah, 61.
BOYNTON, David Atherton, 19.
Edmund, 10.
Everett, 80.
Henry, 37.
BRACKETT, Jeffrey Richardson, 64.
BRADBURY, Horace Dennison, 51.
John Merrill, 11.
BRADFORD, Charles Frederick, 38.
Joseph Russell, 56.

CHAMBERLAYNE,
Charles Frederic, 80b.
CHAMBRÉ, Albert St. John, 64.
CHAMPLIN, John Denison, Jr., 121.
CHAMPNEY, Addison Weld, 109.
George Mather, 10.
Samuel Trowbridge, 106.
CHANDLER, George, 20.
Seth, 91.
William Eaton, 68.
CHANNING, Walter, 80a.
CHAPIN, Alonzo Bowen, 12.
Edwin Hubbell, 106.
Nathaniel Gates, 28.
CHAPMAN, Frederick William, 19.
CHARNOCK, Richard Stephen, 110.
CHASE, Charles Augustus, 80.
Franklin, 107.
George Bigelow, 40.
George Wingate, 23.
James Morss, 11.
Jotham Gould, 36.
Jotham Sewall, 35.
Thomas, 80b.
William Henry, 10.
(See CHACE.)
CHAUNCEY, Charles, 68.
Elihu, 72.
Nathaniel, 91, 127.
William, 93.
CHENEY. Benjamin Pierce, 42.
CHESTER, Joseph Lemuel, 111.
CHICKERING, Benjamin, 22.
Thomas Edward, 47.
CHILD, Addison, 9.
Daniel Franklin, 43.
Dudley Richards, 42.
Isaac, 4.
CHILSON, Gardner, 47. [96.
CHIPMAN, Richard Manning.
CHOATE, Rufus, 82.
CHURCH, Henry Augustus, 64.
Samuel, 96.
CHURCHILL, Gardner Asaph, 70.
CLAFLIN, William, 44.
CLAPP, David, 33.
Ebenezer, 50.
Otis, 44.
William Warland, Jr., 21.
CLARK, Aaron, 101.
Arthur March, 71.
Arthur March Pius, 71.
Benjamin Cutler, 72.
David Oakes, 55.
Edmund Sanford, 71.
Edward Warren, 25.
Frank Gray, 72.

CLARK (Cont'd).
George Faber, 30, 100.
Henry, 11.
Henry Grafton, 28.
James Wilson, 13.
John, 35.
John Taylor, 56.
Jonas Gilman, 71.
Joshua Victor Hopkins, 99.
Luther, 60.
Oliver Richardson, 63.
Randolph Marshall, 34.
Sereno Dickinson, 53.
William Smith, 49.
CLARKE, Dorus, 25.
George Kuhn, 60.
Henry Martyn, 40.
Henry Steele, 104.
Hovey Kilburn, 101.
James Freeman, 22.
James William, 71.
Robert, 115.
Samuel Curtis, 34.
Samuel Fulton, 98.
Thomas William, 54.
CLAY, Henry, 83.
CLEAVELAND, Charles Douglas, 17.
Charles Harley, 105.
CLEVELAND, Charles Dexter, 105.
Edmund Janes, 66.
CLIFFORD, Nathan, 86.
COBB, Samuel Crocker, 23.
William Henry, 76.
COBURN, Daniel Jennings, 17.
Ethan Nelson, 48.
COCHRANE, Gerry Whiting, 47.
CODMAN, Arthur, 61.
Arthur Amory, 61.
George Calvin, 70.
Ogden, 26.
Robert, 27.
COFFIN, Charles Carleton, 31.
Joshua, 90.
Nathaniel Wheeler, 4.
William Edward, 44, 66.
COGGESHALL, William Turner, 111.
COGSWELL, Edward Russell, 50.
George, 53.
John Bear Doane, 58.
Joseph Green, 104.
William, 92.
COLBURN, Charles, 30.
Jeremiah, 17.
COLBY, Harrison Gray Otis, 5.
COLEMAN, Lyman, 115.
COLESWORTHY, Daniel Clement, 8.
COLTON, Chauncey, 95.
Reuben, 80b.

COMSTOCK, William Ogilvie, 29.
CONANT, Arnold William, 10.
Charles Francis, 68.
Ezra, 66.
CONGAR, Samuel Hays, 100.
CONNOLLY, Arthur Theodore, 78.
CONTÉ, Joseph André Casimir, 118.
CONVERSE, Elisha Slade, 47.
James Cogswell, 47.
James Wheaton, 47.
Joshua Perkins, 20.
COOK, Henry, 51.
COOKE, George Willis, 69.
Henry Allen, 64.
Joseph Jesse, 54.
COOLIDGE, Austin Jacobs, 21.
COOPER, Peter, 101.
COOTE, Charles Henry, 122.
COPE, Gilbert, 110.
COPELAND, Elisha, 17.
COPLEY, John Singleton, 81.
COPP, Joseph Addison, 18.
CORDNER, John, 78, 107.
COREY, Deloraine Pendre, 29.
CORLISS, Augustus Whittemore, 118.
CORNELL, William Mason, 14, 42, 107.
COTHREN, William, 94.
COWLES, William Wade, 8, 29.
COWLEY, Charles, 39.
CRAFT, George, 39.
CRAFTS, William Francis, 61.
CRANCH, William, 82.
CRANDALL, Hiram Burr, 30.
CRANE, Andrew Fuller, 103.
Denzell Mansfield, 20.
John Calvin, 77.
Joshua Eddy, 33.
Silas Axtell, 44.
CREECH, Samuel Walley, Jr., 31.
CREHORE, Charles Frederic, 80a.
CROCKER, Alvah, 38, 80a.
Samuel Leonard, 52.
Uriel, 12.
Uriel Haskell, 79.
CROLLALANZA, Jean Baptiste de (Chevalier), 121.
CROMBIE, William Augustus, 80a.
CROOKS, James Warham, 16.
CROSBY, James, 98.
Nathan, 31.
CROSWELL, Andrew, 30.
CROZIER, Hiram Parker, 107.
CRUFT, George Theodore, 72.
CUDWORTH, Warren Handel, 21.

DUYCKINCK, Evert Augustus, 100.
George Long, 100.
DWIGHT, Benjamin Woodbridge, 115.
Theodore. 106.
Theodore Frelinghuysen, 76.
DYER, Ebenezer Porter, 31.

EARL, Hezekiah, 23.
EARLE, Pliny, 73.
EASTMAN, Albert Lorenzo, 70.
Ambrose, 38.
Edmund Tucker, 18.
Lucius Root, 29.
EATON, Arthur Wentworth Hamilton, 75.
John, 126.
Lilley, 43, 95.
Warren Everett, 40.
EDDY, Caleb, 4.
Richard, Jr., 104.
Robert Henry, 52.
EDES, Henry Herbert, 35.
EDGERLY, James Albert, 60.
EDMANDS, Thomas Franklin, 78.
EDWARDS, Henry, 32.
Jonathan, 62.
Tryon, 95.
EGGLESTON, Edward, 124.
EGLE, William Henry, 122.
ELA, Richard, 80b.
Walter, 80b.
ELDER, Charles Ronello, 64.
Janus Granville, 55.   [20.
ELDRIDGE, John Seabury, 125.
ELIOT, Ellsworth, 125.
Samuel Atkins, 4.
William Greenleaf, 106.
ELLERY, Harrison, 28.
ELLIOT, George Perkins, 55.
ELLIOTT, George Millard, 51.
ELLIS, Charles Mayo, 5.
John Harvard, 23.
Rowland, 71.
Sumner, 30.
Warren Bartlett, 78.
William Smith, 114.
ELTON, Romeo, 93.
ELY, William. 92.
EMERSON, And, 17.
Warren, 56.
EMERY, Francis Faulkner, 62.
George Edwin, 39.
Isaac, 25.
John Simpson, 59.
Samuel Hopkins, 66, 101.
William Henry, 58.
EMMONS, Stephen, 20.
ENDICOTT, Charles, 30.
Charles Moses, 94.

ENDICOTT (Cont'd).
Edward Marion, 25.
Eugene Francis, 57.
Frederic, 80.
George Monroe, 55.
William, Jr., 45.
William Ellis, 61.
ENGELHARDT, Conrad, 115.
ENSIGN, Charles Sidney, 77.
ESTABROOKS, John Russell, 116.
ESTY, Constantine Canaris, 56.
EUSTIS, William Tracy, 73.
EVANS,(D'Oyley)John Henry, 125; 127.
EVERETT, Edward, 3.
Edward Franklin, 21.
George Henry, 34.
Percival Lowell, 27.
EWER, Charles, 1.
Peter Folger, 93.

FABENS, Francis Alfred, 103.
FAIRBANKS, Horace, 63.
Stephen, 30.
FAHNESTOCK, George Wolff, 115, 127.
FALES, Henry Edwin, 62.
Stephen, 91.
FARISH, Greggs Joseph, 110.
FARLEY, Frederick Augustus, 107.
FARLOW, Charles Frederic, 67.
FARNHAM, Luther, 12, 62.
FARNSWORTH, Ezra, 42.
Ezra, Jr., 71.
James Delap, 92.
FARNUM, Darius Daniels, 35.
FARRAR, Timothy, 7, 84.
FARRINGTON, Ebenezer Trescott, 46.
FARWELL, John Whittemore, 62.
Stephen Thurston, 9.
FAUNCE, Walter Hamlet, 65.
FAWCETT, Alfred, 49.
FEARING, Albert, 5, 39.
Andrew Coatsworth, Jr., 71.
FELLOWS, Charles Sumner, 26, 119.
George Marshall, 78.
FELT, Joseph Barlow, 6, 84, 89.
FELTON, Cornelius Conway, 84.
FENNO, John Brooks, 53.
FESSENDEN, Francis, 70.
Guy Mannering. 92.
John Milton, 68.
FIELD, David Dudley, 95.
Henry Martyn, 108.
Osgood, 115.

FIELD (Cont'd).
Walbridge Abner, 80a.
William Evarts, 69.
FILLMORE, Millard, 84, 90.
(See PHILLIMORE.)
FINOTTI, Joseph Maria, 34.
FIRTH, Abraham, 33.
FISH, Benjamin, 113.
James Dean, 112.
FISHER, Alvin Lane, 42.
Aron Estey, 19.
George Purnell, 112.
Warren, Jr., 47.
FISKE, Andrew, 80
George Jenckes, 31.
FITTS, James Hill, 34.
FLANDERS, Henry, 108.
FLETCHER, Calvin, 109,127.
FLINT, Charles Louis, 36.
Charles Louis, Jr., 71.
David Boardman, 64.
FOGG, Francis Brinley, 104.
John Samuel Hill, 18.
John Smith, 46.
FOLEY, William James, 33.
FOLGER,William Coleman.67.
FOLSOM, Albert Alonzo, 61.
George, 91.
FOOTE, Elial Todd, 92.
Henry Wilder, 69.
FORBES, John Murray, 67.
Robert Bennett, 43.
FORMAN, Jacob Gilbert, 107.
FORSAITH,Francis Flint.70.
FORSTER, Edward Jacob,31.
FORSYTH, Francis Flint, 70.
Frederic Gregory, 62.
FOSTER, Dudley, 60.
Ebenezer Brewer, 29.
Herman, 50.
John, 38.
Joseph, 123.
William, 22.
Wilham Eaton, 62.
(See FORSTER.)
FOWLE, William Bentley, 26.
FOWLER, Frank Field, 28.
Moses Field, 28.
Samuel Page, 25.
William Chauncey, 27.
FOX, Gustavus Vasa, 55.
John Lawrence, 16.
FRANCIS, Convers, 93.
John Wakefield. 100.
FREELAND, Charles William, 40.
FREEMAN, Edward Augustus, 87, 124.
FRENCH, Aaron Davis Weld, 68.
Benjamin Vinton, 2.
Eli, 102.
Francis, 29.
Francis Ormond, 68.

HARBACH, William Francis, 75.
HARBAUGH, Henry, 101.
HARDEN, William, 124.
HARDING, Francis Low, 17.
George Warren, 47.
Willard Mason, 19.
HARDWICK, Benjamin Cutler, 71.
HARDY, John Henry, 60.
HARMAN, Samuel Bickerton, 98.
HARRINGTON, Leonard Bond, 47.
HARRIS, Benjamin Winslow, 33.
Caleb Fiske, 44.
Edward Doubleday, 67.
Luther Metcalf, 9.
Robert William, 115.
Thomas Burdett, 20.
William Thaddeus, 3.
HARROD, Henry, 99.
HART, Charles Henry, 113.
HARTER, David, 105.
HARVEY, Matthew, 16.
Moses, 120.
Peter, 41.
HARWOOD, Herbert Joseph, 80.
HASKELL, Daniel Noyes, 12.
HASKINS, David Greene, 38.
David Greene, Jr., 38.
John, 11.
Ralph, 5, 55.
HASSAM, John Tyler, 34.
HASTINGS, Walter, 50.
HATCH, Jarvis Malatiah, 110.
HATHEWAY, Simon William, 58.
HAUGHTON, James, 47.
(See HOUGHTON.)
HAVEN, Franklin, 13.
Henry Philemon, 40.
Samuel Foster, 89.
HAWES, Frank Mortimer, 77.
HAWKES, Ezra, 49.
HAWKINS, Alfred, 98.
HAWKS, John Milton, 54.
HAWLEY, Charles, 123.
Elias Sill, 11.
HAYDEN, Henry Cornelius, 60.
Henry Rogers, 75.
Horace Edwin, 117.
William, 5.
HAYES, Charles Wells, 58, 122.
Francis Brown, 18.
John Lord, 62.
Rutherford Birchard, 86.
Stephen Hobbs, 58.
Thomas McCullock, 35.
William Allen, 2d, 74.
HAYNES, Guy Carleton, 8.

HAYWARD, Elijah, 98.
Isaac Davenport, 36.
(See HEYWOOD.)
HAZARD, Rowland, 44.
Samuel, 97.
HAZEN, Henry Allen, 56.
Thomas Joseph, 18.
HEALY, John Plummer, 10.
HEARD, John, 44.
John Trull, 29.
(See HURD.)
HEBARD, Learned, 42.
HENRY, Matthew Schropp, 110.
HENSHAW, Daniel, 17, 110.
David, 83.
George Eddy, 18.
John, 2.
Joseph Lyman, 32.
Joshua Sidney, 105.
HEPWORTH, George Hughes, 22.
HERSEY, Alfred Cushing, 66.
Alfred Henry, 61.
HEWINS, Charles Amasa, 49.
HEYWOOD, John Healy, 106.
William Sweetser, 74.
(See HAYWARD.)
HIGGINSON, Thomas Wentworth, 37.
Waldo, 3, 68.
HILDEBURN, Charles Riché, 119.
Charles Swift Riché, 119.
HILDRETH, Henry Orin, 24.
Samuel Prescott, 92.
HILL, Clement Hugh, 43.
Don Gleason, 65.
Edward Judkins, 31.
Hamilton Andrews, 45.
James Edward Radford, 74.
John, 47.
Thomas, 85.
HILLS, George Morgan, 125.
HILTON, Gustavus Arthur, 76.
William, 20.
HINCKS, Edward Winslow, 50.
William Bliss, 54.
HINDS, Calvin Parkman, 18.
HINMAN, Royal Ralph, 93.
HITCHCOCK, John, 79.
HOADLY, Charles Jeremy, 91.
HOAR, George Frisbie, 73.
John Emory, 33.
Samuel, 82.
HOBART, Henry Linsley, 32.
Peter, Jr., 21.
HOBBS, Frederick, 95.
HOCKEY, Joseph, 21.
HODGES, Almon Danforth, 10.
Almon Danforth, Jr., 78.
Edward Fuller, 4.
Richard Manning, 30.

HODGMAN, Edwin Ruthven, 17.
HOES, Roswell Randall, 120.
HOLDEN, Austin Wells, 114.
Edward, 16.
Frederic Augustus, 110.
Luther Loud, 45.
HOLLAND, Frederick West, 20.
Henry Ware, 56.
HOLLEY, Alexander Hamilton, 41.
HOLLIS, Benjamin Pratt, 21.
William Thomas, 36.
HOLME, John Stanford, 105.
HOLMES, Howland, 55.
Lemuel Le Baron, 76.
(See HOMES.)
HOLTON, David Parsons, 37.
HOMANS, Charles Dudley, 40.
Isaac Smith, 108.
John, 2d, 80a.
HOMES, Henry Augustus, 114.
HOOKER, Anson Parker, 36.
HOOPER, John, 28.
Nathaniel Leech, 74.
Robert, 35.
Robert, Jr., 32.
Samuel, 14.
Samuel Hooper, 80a.
Thomas, Jr., 80b.
HOPKINSON, Thomas, 11.
HOPPIN, Nicholas, 26.
HORNBLOWER, Joseph Courten, 94.
HORNE, Edwin Temple, 66.
HORSFORD, Eben Norton, 23.
HOSMER, Charles Edward, 63.
George Washington, 106.
HOTCHKISS, Frank Edwin, 54.
HOUGH, Franklin Benjamin, 108.
HOUGHTON, Henry Oscar, 71.
William Stevens, 46.
(See HAUGHTON.)
HOWARD, Cecil Hampden Cutts, 125.
John Seaver, 28.
Joseph Jackson, 101.
HOWE, Appleton, 33.
Archibald Murray, 80.
Elijah Franklin, 63.
Joseph, 104.
Theodore Lyman, 6.
HOWELL, George Rogers, 114.
HOWLAND, Asa, 24.
John, 91.
John Andrews, 92.

PALMER, Albert, 68.
Joseph, 9.
PARK, Edwards Amasa, 48.
PARKE, Benjamin, 114.
PARKER, Augustus, 39.
Daniel Pinckney, 4, 83.
David McCanie, 55.
Foxhall Alexander, 117.
Francis Jewett, 41.
Francis Vose, 51.
Henry Ainsworth, 72.
Isaac, 13.
James, 26.
John Wells, 8.
Leonard Moody, 96.
Samuel Trask, 26.
Willard, 123.
William Albert, 52.
William Prentiss, 76.
PARKMAN, Francis, 32.
PARSONS, Charles William, 64.
Samuel Holden, 89, 127.
Theophilus, 22.
Thomas William, 29.
Usher, 30, 89.
William, 5, 94.
PATCH, Ira Joseph, 79.
PATTEN, Claudius Buchanan, 23.
PATTERSON, Albert Clarke, 32.
David Williams, 113.
George Herbert, 78, 117.
PAVER, William, 102.
PAYEN — PAYNE, James Bertrand, 105.
PAYSON, John Phillips, 53.
Samuel Russell, 40.
PEABODY, Andrew Preston, 67.
George, 83.
William Smith, 35.
PEACOCK, Edward, 103.
PEARSON, Jonathan, 99.
Linus Everett, 75.
Thomas Scott, 12.
PEASE, Austin Spencer, 33.
David Harlow, 111.
Frederic Salmon, 96.
PEASLEE, Charles Hazen, 12.
PECHELL, Hervey Charles, 118.
PECK, Asahel, 37.
Ira Ballou, 10.
John Mason, 94.
Thomas Bellows, 56.
PECKER, Jonathan Eastman, 68.
PEET, Stephen Denison, 121.
PEIRCE, Benjamin Osgood, 59.
Ebenezer Weaver, 23.
Jonathan, 18.
Joshua Winslow, 40.

PEIRCE (Cont'd).
William, 21, 64.
(See PIERCE.)
PENHALLOW, Charles Sherburne, 80a.
Pearce Wentworth, 60.
PENNELL, Robert Franklin, 62.
PERKINS, Augustus Thorndike, 29.
Frederic Beecher, 52, 111.
George Augustus, 62.
Horatio Nelson, 51.
Samuel Clarke, 106.
William, 44.
William Edward, 43.
PERLEY, Ira, 38.
Sidney, 60.
PERRY, Gardner Braman, 15.
Oliver Hazard, 35.
Oliver Henry, 41.
William Stevens, 116.
PETERS, George Haswell, 46.
William Cowper, 46.
PETTIGREW, William Jay, 64.
PETTUS, William Jerdone, 80a.
PHELPS, Abner, 3.
Ansel, Jr., 94.
Franklin Stiles, 59.
Noah Amherst, 93.
Samuel Wright, 94.
Sylvester, 30.
PHILBRICK, John Dudley, 18.
PHILLIMORE, William Phillimore Watts, 126.
(See FILLMORE.)
PHILLIPPS, Thomas (Sir), 85.
PHILLIPS, Calvin Tilden, 63.
Elijah Brigham, 78.
Henry, Jr., 121.
Jonathan, 82.
Stephen Henry, 77.
Stephen Willard, 79.
William, 15.
PHŒNIX, Stephen Whitney, 114.
PICKERING, Henry White, 33.
James Farrington, 71.
PIERCE, Edward Lillie, 73.
Frederic Beech, 60.
Frederick Clifton, 59.
Henry Lillie, 42.
John, 81.
Roger Newton, 10.
(See PEIRCE.)
PIKE, James Shephard, 60.
Richard, 20.
PIPER, Solomon, 29.
PITKIN, Timothy, 83.

PITMAN, Stephen Minot, 57.
PITTS, Richard, 9.
PLIMPTON, Moses, 9.
PLUMB, Albert Hale, 34.
PLUMER, Avery. 47.
William, Jr., 89.
POLAND, Luke Potter, 37.
POLLARD, George Edward, 80b.
POMEROY, Benjamin, 105.
POOLE, William Frederick, 122.
POOR, Alfred, 9.
John Alfred, 48.
John Augustus, 68.
POORE, Alfred, 9.
POPE, Charles Greenwood, 43.
Charles Henry, 74.
Franklin Leonard, 74.
Lemuel, 34.
William, 40.
PORTER, Alexander Sylvanus, 57.
Edward Griffin, 48.
George Washington, 116.
James Madison, 106.
Joseph Whitcom, 54.
Josiah, 24.
William Smith, 93.
POTTER, Chandler Eastman, 97.
Charles Francis, 70.
Elisha Reynolds, 92.
Moses, 23.
POTTS, Thomas Maxwell, 126.
William John, 117.
POWELL, Charles Thuillier Mallapert, 75.
POWERS, Herman, 12.
PRATT, Edward Ellerton, 70.
Eleazer Franklin, 7.
Francis Greenleaf, Jr., 78.
George Williams, 45.
Robert Marion, 75.
Sereno Brainard, 69.
Stillman, 25.
Stillman Baxter, 68.
PREBLE, George Henry, 33.
Henry Oxnard, 47.
PREMIO REAL, El Conde de, 120.
PRENDERGAST, John Patrick, 114.
PRENTISS, Henry James, 19.
John, 89.
PRESCOTT, Alfred Abbott, 16.
Frederick William, 8.
George Jarvis, 72.
George Watson, 36.
Nathan Bean, 27.
William, 95.
William Hickling, 82.
PRESTON, James Willard, 60.
Jonathan, 47.

SAUNDERS, Charles Hicks, 73.
William Augustus, 23.
SAVAGE, William, 5.
SAWTELL, William Henry, 50.
SAWYER, Frederic William, 29.
George Augustus, 80*a*.
Nathaniel, 98.
Samuel Elwell, 49.
Timothy Thompson, 69.
SAYWARD, Charles Augustus, 68.
SCHARF, John Thomas, 119.
SCHOULER, James, 73.
SCHROEDER, John Frederick, 102.
SCOTT, Benjamin, 114.
Martin Bowen, 112.
SCUDDER, Henry Austin, 17.
SCULL, Gideon Delaplaine,117.
SEARS, David, 81.
George Oliver, 22.
Joshua Montgomery, 65.
Philip Howes, 13.
Richard Willard, 59.
SEDGWICK, Charles Frederick, 93.
SERGEANT, Thomas, 83.
SETON, Robert (Mgr.), 122.
SEVER, James Warren, 40.
SEWALL, Benjamin, 46.
Charles Chauncy, 23.
Joseph, 82.
Samuel, 90.
SHARPLES, Stephen Paschall, 74.
SHATTUCK, George Cheyne, 68, 82.
George Otis, 80.
Lemuel, 1.
SHAW, Henry Russell, 67.
Lemuel, 82.
Robert Gould, 82.
SHEA, John Dawson, 105.
John Gilmary, 87, 105.
SHEDD, Abraham Dailey, 35.
Frank Edson, 79.
SHEFFIELD, George, 69.
SHELDON, George, 121.
Henry Olcott, 90.
Hezekiah Spencer, 73.
SHEPARD, Charles Augustus Billings, 26.
SHEPLEY, Stephen, 56.
SHEPPARD, Edward Naman, 61.
John Hannibal, 24.
SHERMAN, Charles Bowker, 18.
SHERWIN, Thomas, 36, 59.
SHILLABER, William Green, 73.

SHIPMAN, Stephen Vaughn, 108.
SHIRLEY, Evelyn Philip, 121.
John Major, 37.
SHREVE, Benjamin, 47.
SHURTLEFF, Benjamin,82.
Nathaniel Bradstreet, 2.
SILLIMAN, Benjamin, 83.
Benjamin, Jr., 94.
SILLOWAY, Thomas William, 20.
SIMMONS, George Arthur, 22.
George Washington, 34.
Stephen Carver, 12.
SIMONDS, Artemas, 6.
SIMS, Clifford Stanley, 110.
Richard, 102.
SKINNER, Charles Augustus, 27.
Francis, 52.
SLACK, Charles Wesley, 57.
Samuel Ruggles, 42, 102.
SLADE, Daniel Denison, 43.
SLAFTER, Carlos, 39.
Edmund Farwell, 25.
SLATER, Nelson, 115.
SLAUGHTER, Philip, 121.
SLEEPER, Jacob, 36.
John Sherburne, 48.
SMALLEY, Elam, 104.
Elijah, 37.
SMETS, Alexander Augustus, 107.
SMITH, Asa Dodge, 41.
Ballard, 97.
Benjamin Greene, 47.
Buckingham, 112.
Charles Perrin, 115.
George, 111.
George Archibald, 125.
George Girdler, 13.
George Plumer, 65.
Henry, 42.
Henry Mitchell, 103.
John Challenor Covington, 123.
John Jay, 109.
John Spear, 100.
Joseph, 86.
Joseph Adams, 52.
Joseph Heber, 58.
Ralph Dunning, 91.
Thomas Buckingham, 112.
Thomas Carter, 4.
William Ballard, 97.
William Henry Leland, 15.
William Rudolph, 100.
William Spooner, 65.
Winfield Scott, 43.
(See SMYTH.)
SMITHETT,   William
Thomas, 18, 107.
SMYTH, Egbert Coffin, 65.
Frederick, 75.

SMYTH (Cont'd).
Ralph Dunning, 91.
Thomas, 100.
SNELLING, George Henry, 59.
SNOW, David, 46.
George Knowles, 67.
Samuel, 62.
SNOWDEN, James Ross, 116.
SOMERBY, Gustavus Adolphus, 27.
Horatio Gates, 2, 107.
SOWDON, Arthur John Clark, 43.
SPALDING, Samuel Jones,23.
SPARHAWK, George, 91.
SPARKS, Jared, 4.
SPAULDING, Solomon Robinson, 45.
SPEARE, Alden, 24.
SPENCER, Richard Pratt, 41.
William Vaughan, 31.
SPOFFORD, John Calvin, 80*b*.
SPOONER, Alden Jermain, 112.
Thomas, 110, 127.
William Brown, 45.
SPRAGUE, Franklin Harvey, 19.
Henry Harrison, 52.
Peleg, 82.
William Buell, 93.
SQUIER, Ephraim George,110.
STACKPOLE, David Dunlap, 43.
STANDISH, Myles, 71.
STANHOPE, Earl, 85.
Philip Henry, 85.
STANLEY, Clinton Warrington, 50.
Timothy Wadsworth, 42.
STANWOOD, Edward, 67.
STAPLES, Carlton Albert, 72.
William Read, 92.
STARBUCK, Alexander, 53.
STARK, James Henry, 74.
STARR, Frank Farnsworth, 70.
STEARNS, Charles, 18.
Charles Augustus, 40.
Eben Sperry, 10, 105.
Edward, 68.
Joseph Barker, 20.
Josiah Atherton, 18.
Oliver, 107.
STEBBINS, Oliver Bliss, 57.
STEDMAN, Charles Harrison, 3.
Daniel Baxter, 47.
STEELE, Benjamin Hinman, 37.
STEINER, Lewis Henry, 124.
STETSON, Caleb, 46.
Eliot Dawes, 77.

Index of Members.

149

WHITAKER, Edgar Kimball, 19.
WHITCOMB, James, 90.
Samuel, Jr., 90.
William Wirt, 16.
WHITE, Albert Smith, 90.
Alden Perley, 77.
Ambrose Haskell, 49.
Andrew Dickson, 88.
Benjamin Franklin, 11.
Charles Harold Evelyn, 125.
Daniel Appleton, 82.
Edward Young, 37.
George, 16.
Henry, 90.
John Gardner, 19.
Joseph, 19.
Pliny Holton, 38.
WHITEHEAD, William Adee, 100.
WHITING, George Augustus, 54.
John Samuel, 63.
Nathaniel, 11.
William, 9.
WHITMAN, Ezekiel, 85.
William, 32.
WHITMORE, Charles Octavius, 28.
William Henry, 12.
WHITNEY, Arthur Eastman, 80b
David Rice, 79.
Frederick Augustus, 10.
Henry Austin, 14.
Thomas Edwin, 92.
WHITTEMORE, Bernard Bemis, 99.
Thomas, 3.
Thomas Jefferson, 13.
WHITTIER, Daniel Bodwell, 60.
John Greenleaf, 37.
WHITWELL, William, 29.
WIGGIN, Andrew, 35.
George Thompson, 57.
John Kimball, 21.
WIGGLESWORTH, George, 80.
WIGHT, Orlando Williams, 106.
William Ward, 74.
WILBOR, Otis, 95.
WILDE, Samuel Sumner, 82.

WILDER, Edward Baker, 74.
James Marshall, 17.
Marshall Pinckney, 7.
Moses Hale, 120.
William Henry, 56.
WILDES, George Dudley, 119.
WILKINS, John Hubbard, 23.
WILKINSON, Ezra, 17.
WILLARD, Joseph, 1.
Moses Thompson, 27.
Paul, Jr., 10.
WILLCUTT, Levi Lincoln, 71.
WILLEY, Tolman, 12.
WILLIAMS, Alexander, 20.
Charles Crosby, 65.
Charles Kilbourne, 90.
Edward Henry, 74.
Eleazer, 90.
Henry, 75.
James Fouquet, 36.
John Fletcher, 116.
Moses, 80.
Statham, 95.
Stephen West, 91.
WILLIAMSON, Joseph, 53.
William Cross, 79.
William Durkee, 91.
WILLIS, Clement, 64.
William, 85, 89.
WILLSON, Edmund Burke, 22.
WILMOT, Robert Duncan, 123.
WILSON, Edward Chase, 30.
Elisha Tyson, 31.
Henry, 21.
John, 76.
John Boynton, 51.
William Martin, 112.
William Woodbridge, 36.
(See WILLSON.)
WINKLEY, Samuel Hobart, 22.
WINSLOW, Almerin Henry, 44.
Charles Frederick, 21.
Edward, 60.
George, 2.
Isaac, 7.
Samuel Wallace, 58.
William Copley, 68.
Winthrop Church, 76.
WINSOR, Justin, 7.

WINTHROP, Robert Charles, 5.
Robert Charles, Jr., 73.
William, 110.
WISE, William Gray, 19, 65.
WITHINGTON, George Gardner, 22.
WOLCOTT, Joshua Huntington, 6.
Roger, 79.
Samuel, 97.
(See WALCOTT.)
WOOD, Isaac Francis, 117.
John, 105.
WOODBURY, Charles Levi, 35.
Levi, 83.
WOODMAN, Cyrus, 34, 101.
WOODS, Henry Ernest, 63.
WOODWARD, Ashbel, 98.
Frederick Francis, 80b.
Royal, 62.
William Elliot, 18.
WOODWELL, Charles Henry, 34.
WOOLDREDGE, John, 46.
WOOLLEY, Charles, 34.
WOOLSON, James Adams, 69.
WORTHINGTON, Erastus, 34.
Roland, 66.
WRIGHT, Carroll Davidson, 58.
Eben, 45.
Edwin, 47.
Frank Vernon, 77.
George Wellman, 77.
John Harvey, 38.
John Stratton, 45.
Joseph Warren, 4.
Thomas, 111.
William James, 77.
WYMAN, Isaac Chauncey, 60.
Rufus, 17.
Thomas Bellows, Jr., 7, 92.
WYNNE, Thomas Hicks, 109.

YORK, Jasper Hazen, 16.
YOUNG, Edward James, 67.
James Holden, 80.

ZABRISKIE, Francis Nicoll, 61.

Index of Places.

.

www.ingramcontent.com/pod-product-compliance
Lightning Source LLC
Chambersburg PA
CBHW030848270326
41928CB00007B/1269